Lacy Sunshine's Portraits Coloring Book

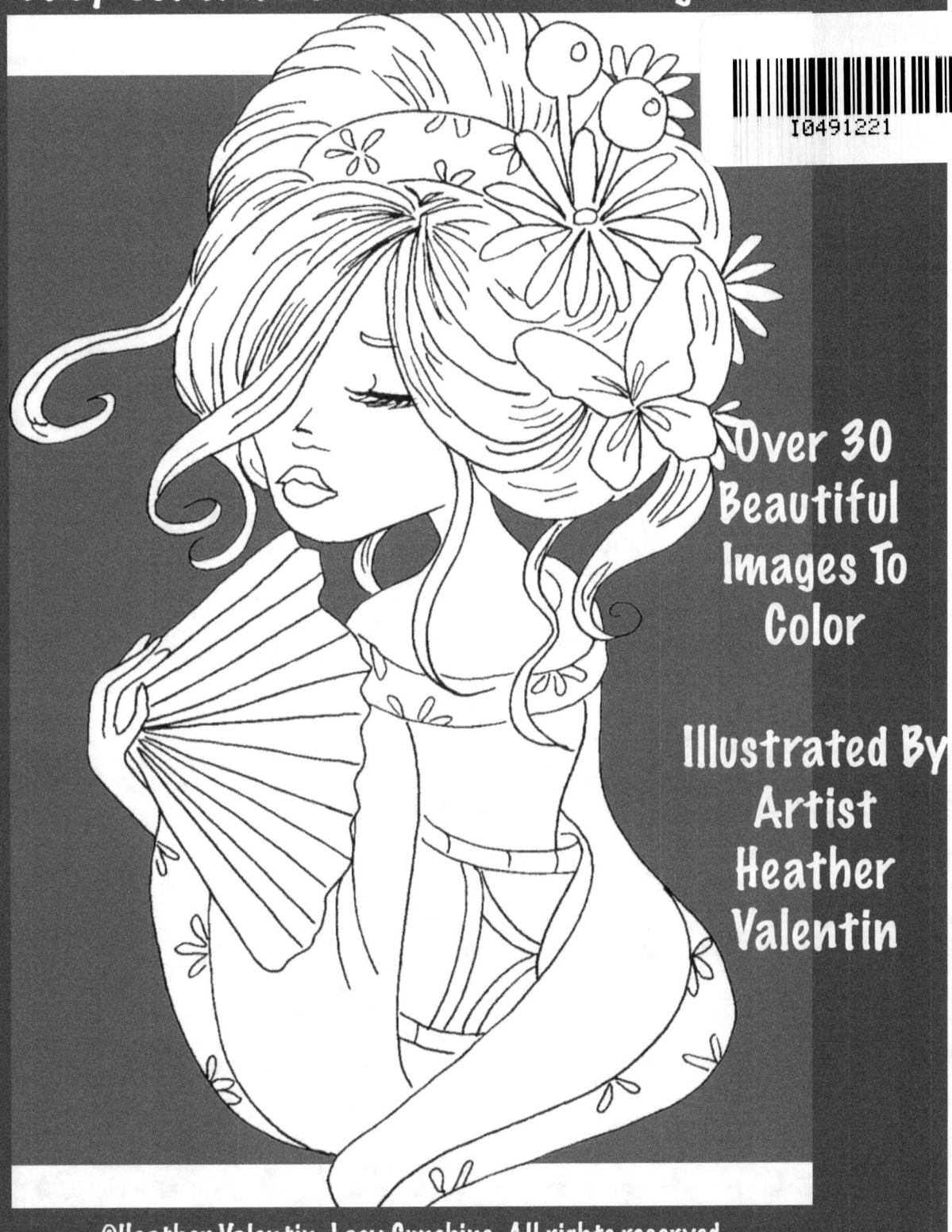

Over 30 Beautiful Images To Color

Illustrated By Artist Heather Valentin

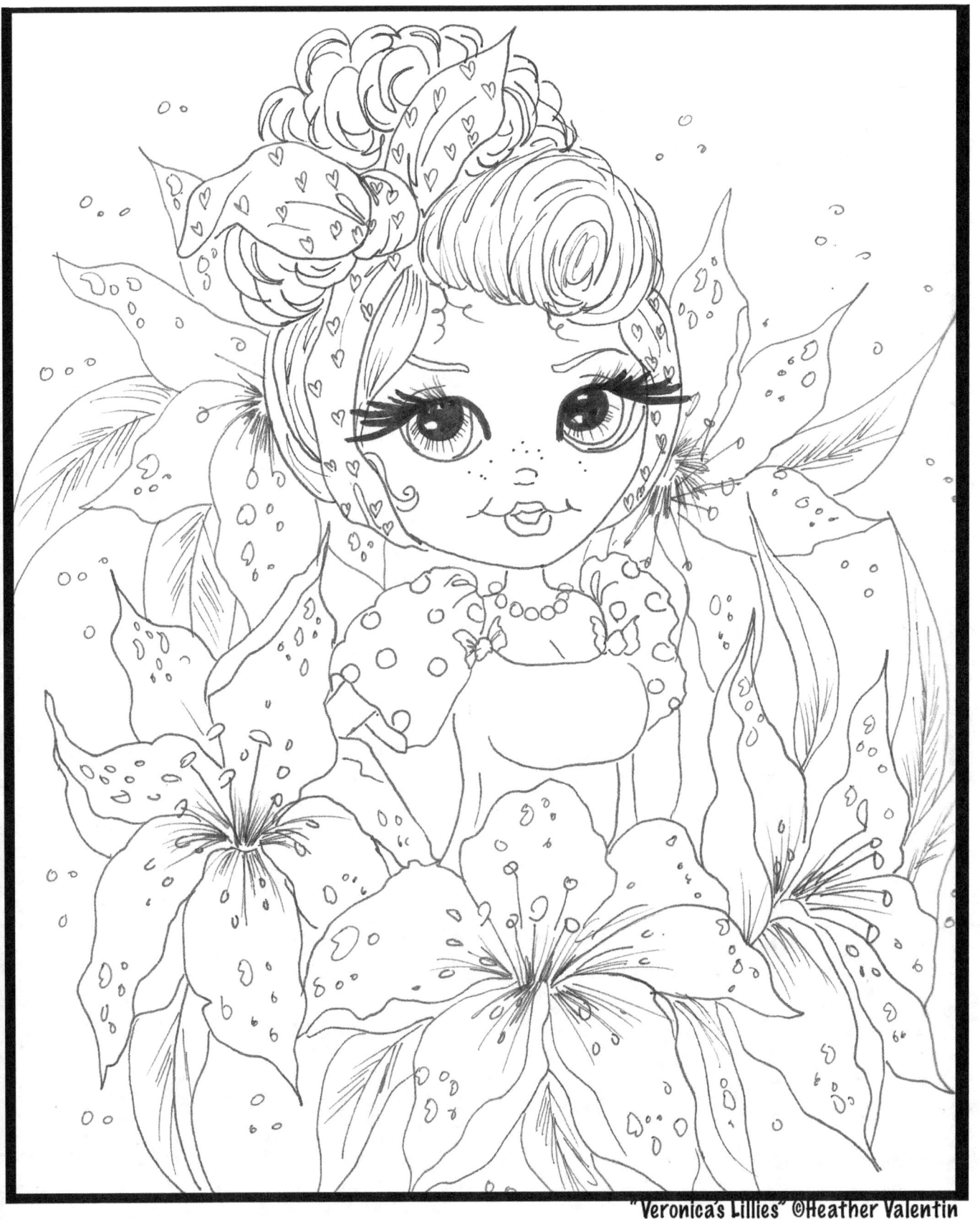

"Veronica's Lillies" ©Heather Valentin

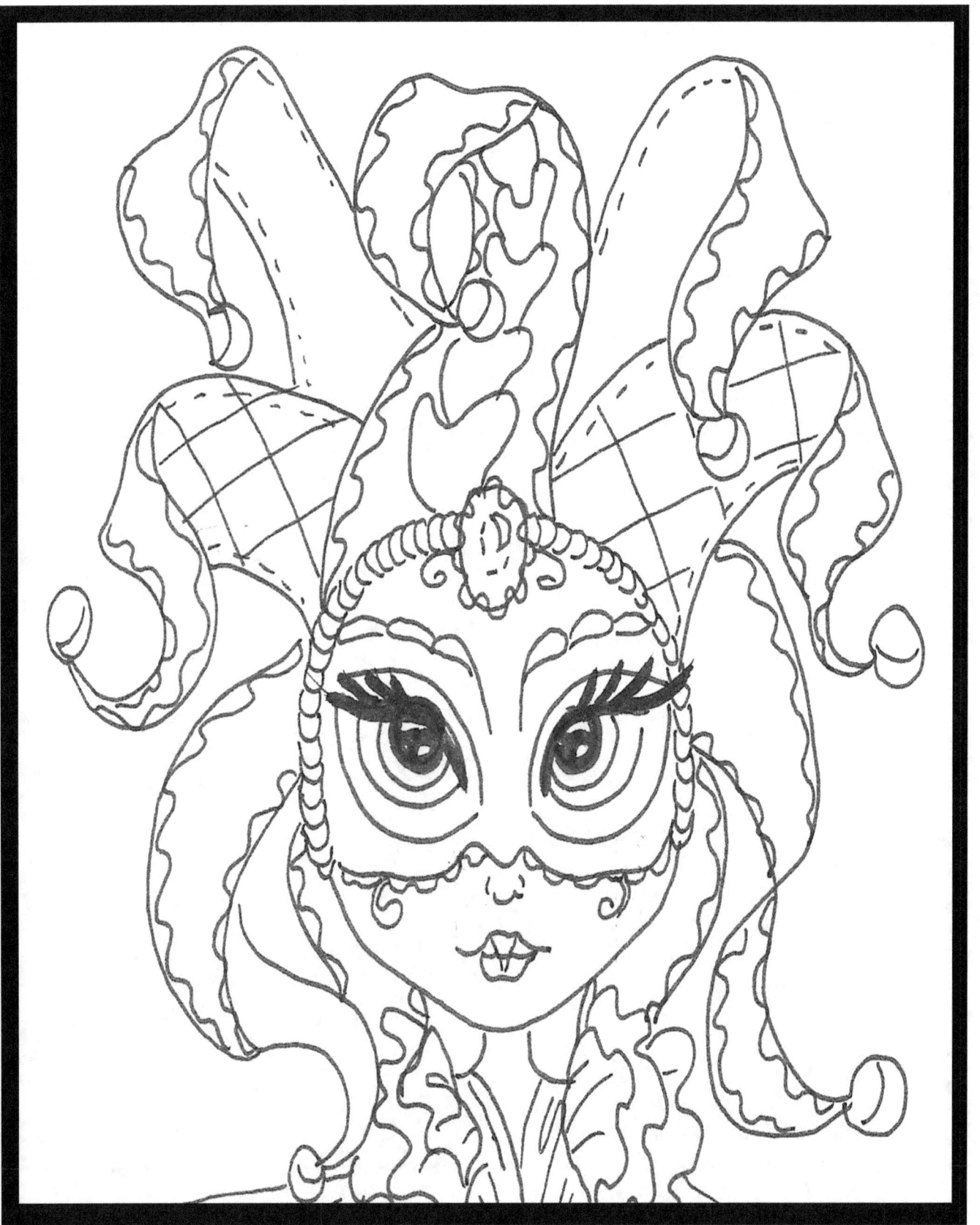

"Marcela" by Heather Valentin

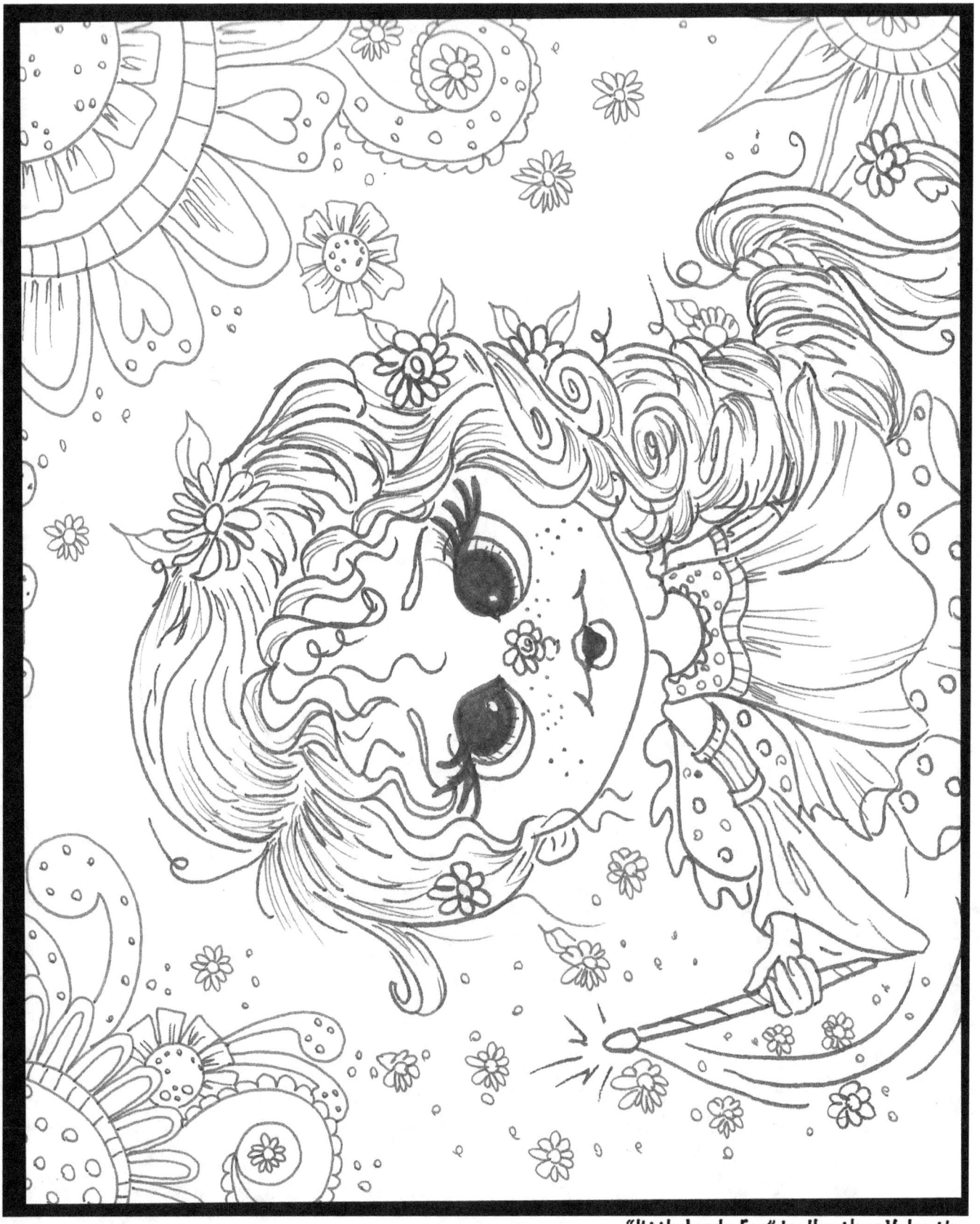

"little Layla Fae" by Heather Valentin

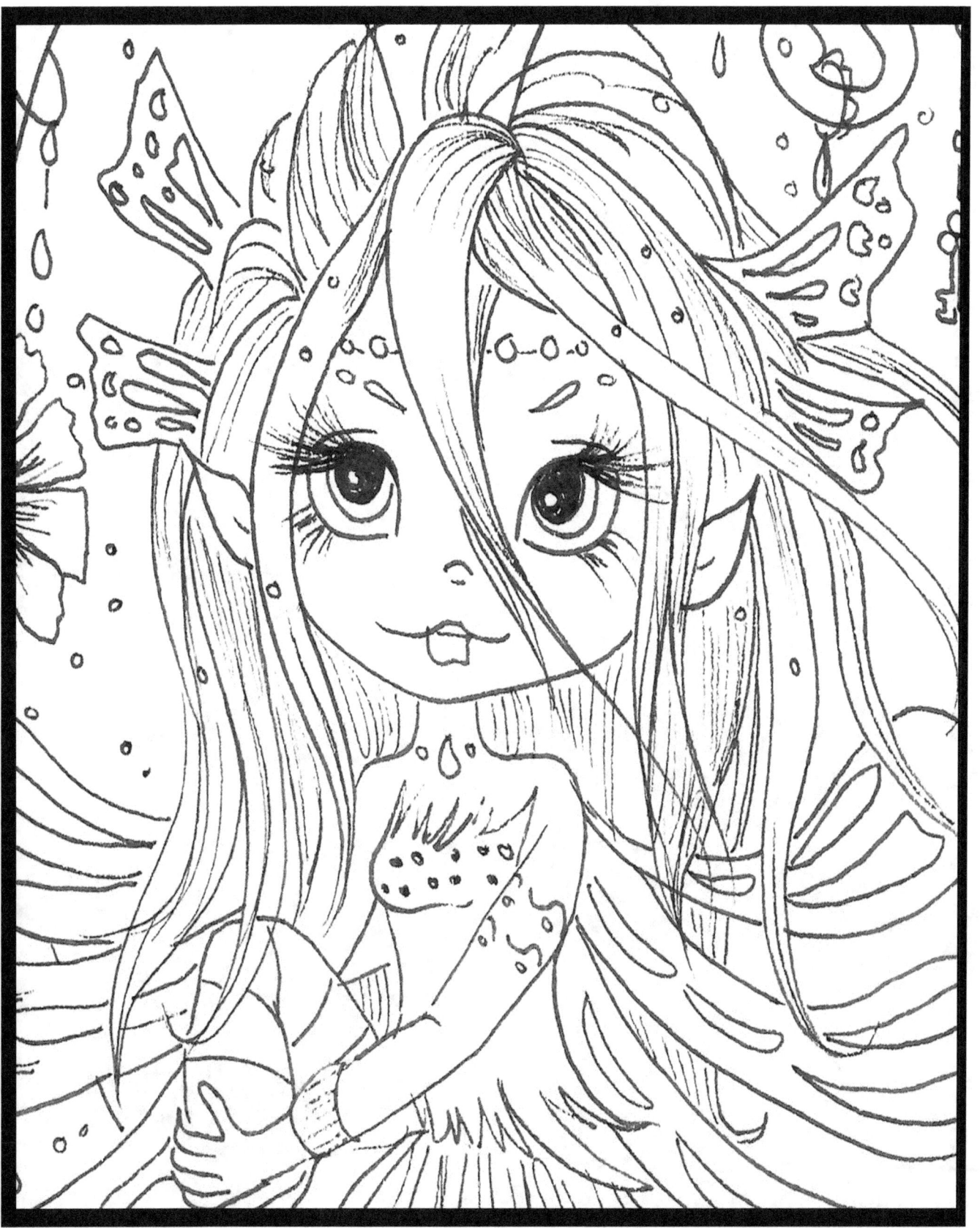

"Mystique" by Heather Valentin

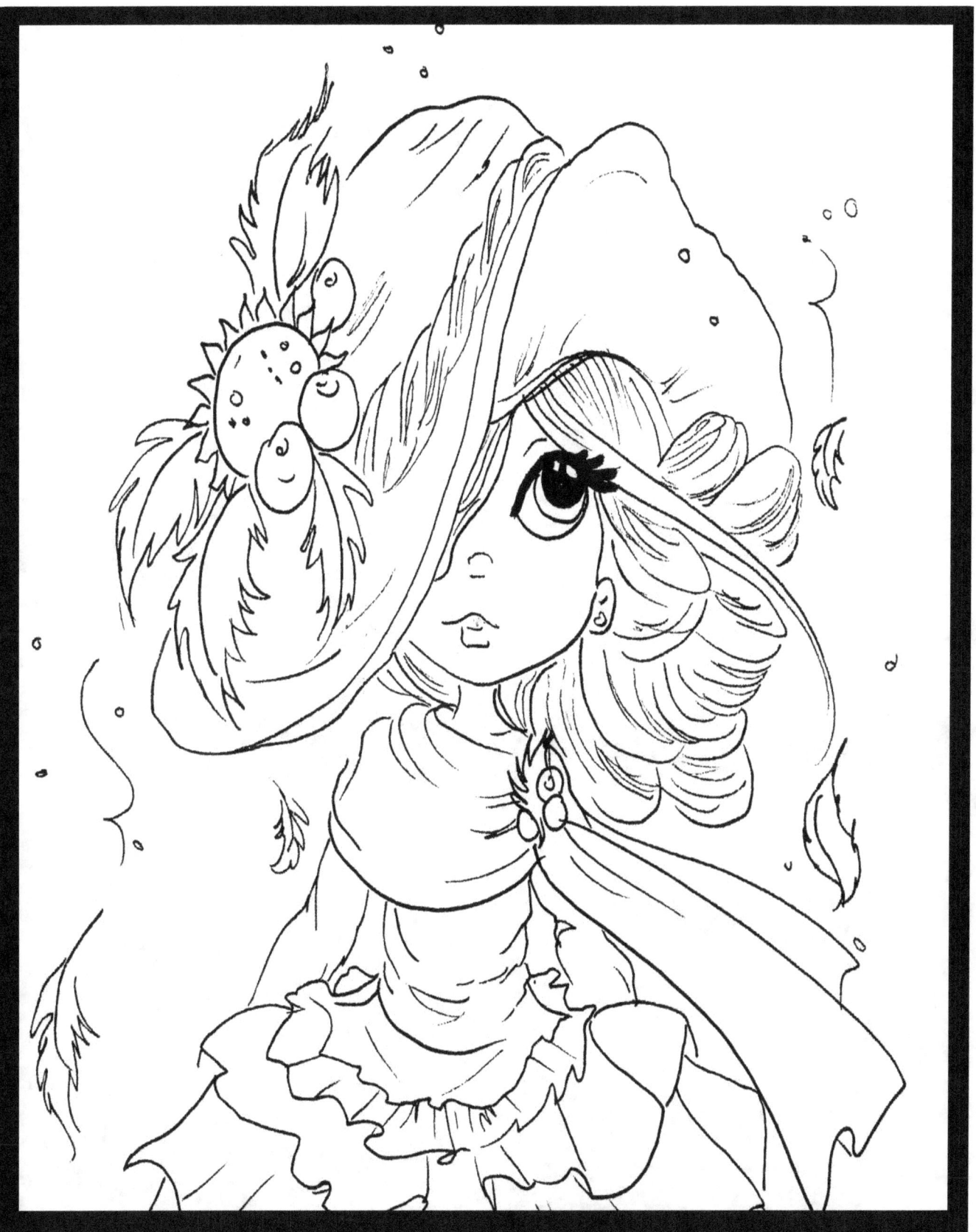

"Jocelyn Moppet" by Heather Valentin

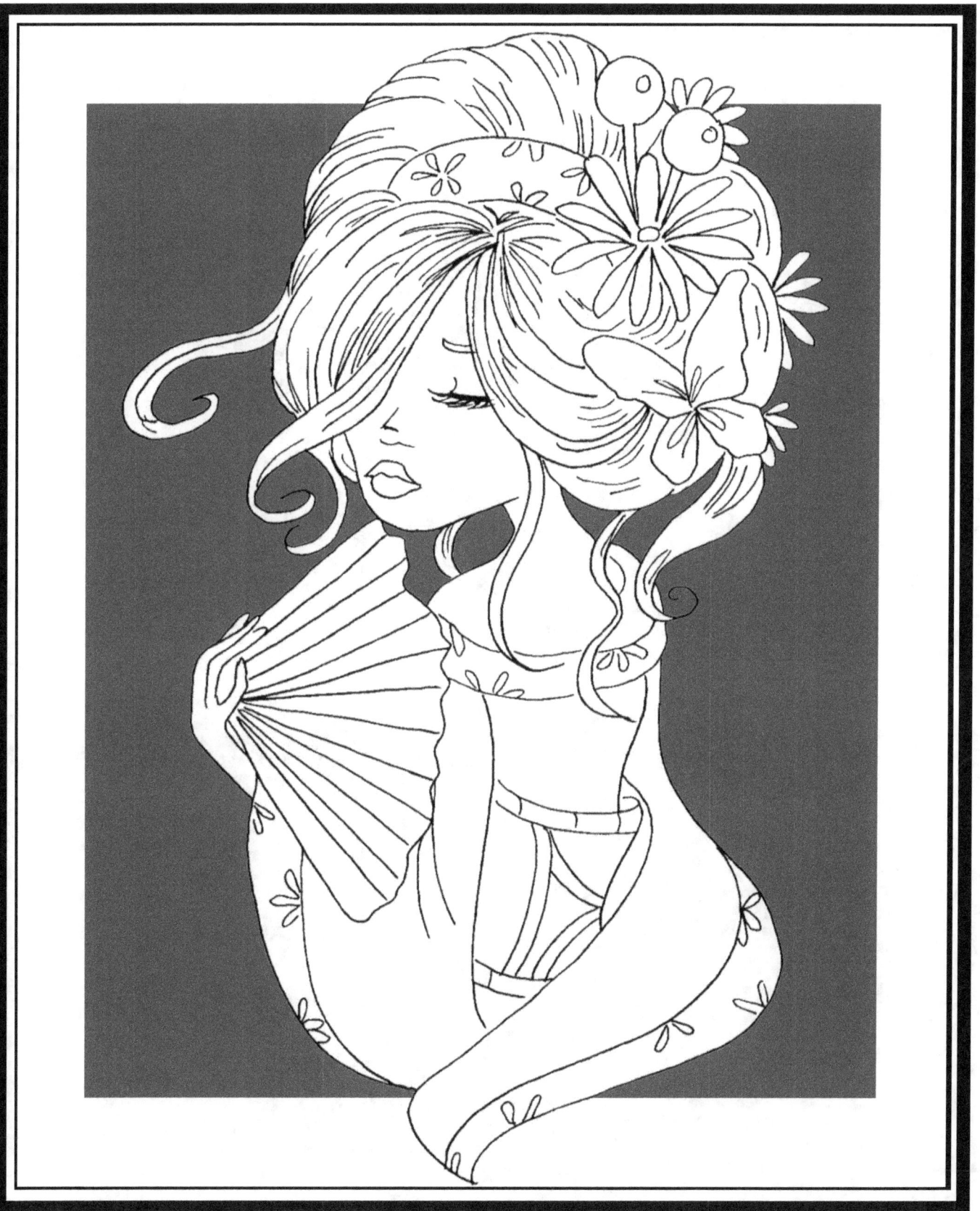

"Keiko" ©Heather Valentin

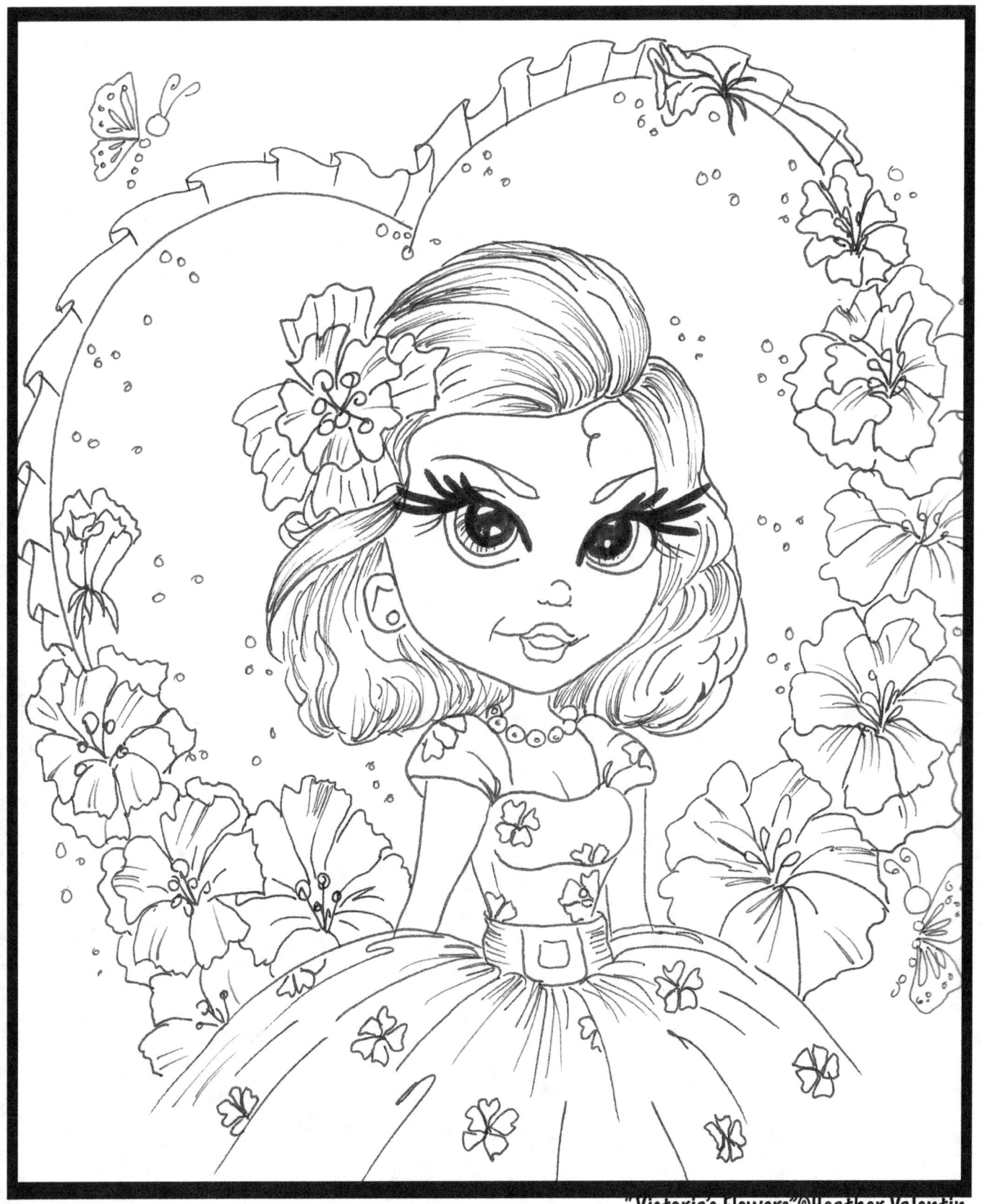

"Victoria's Flowers" ©Heather Valentin

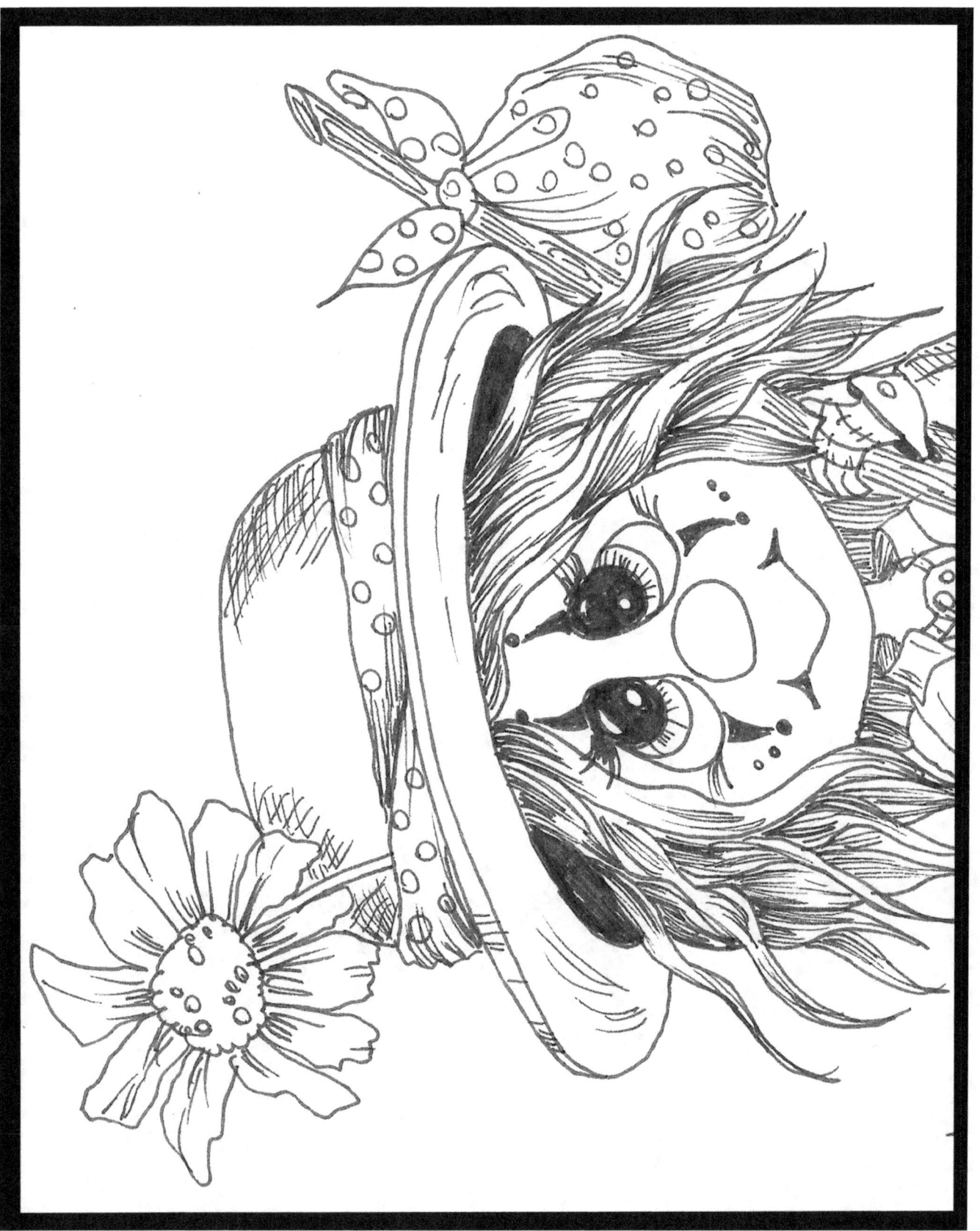

"Bowbo" by Heather Valentin

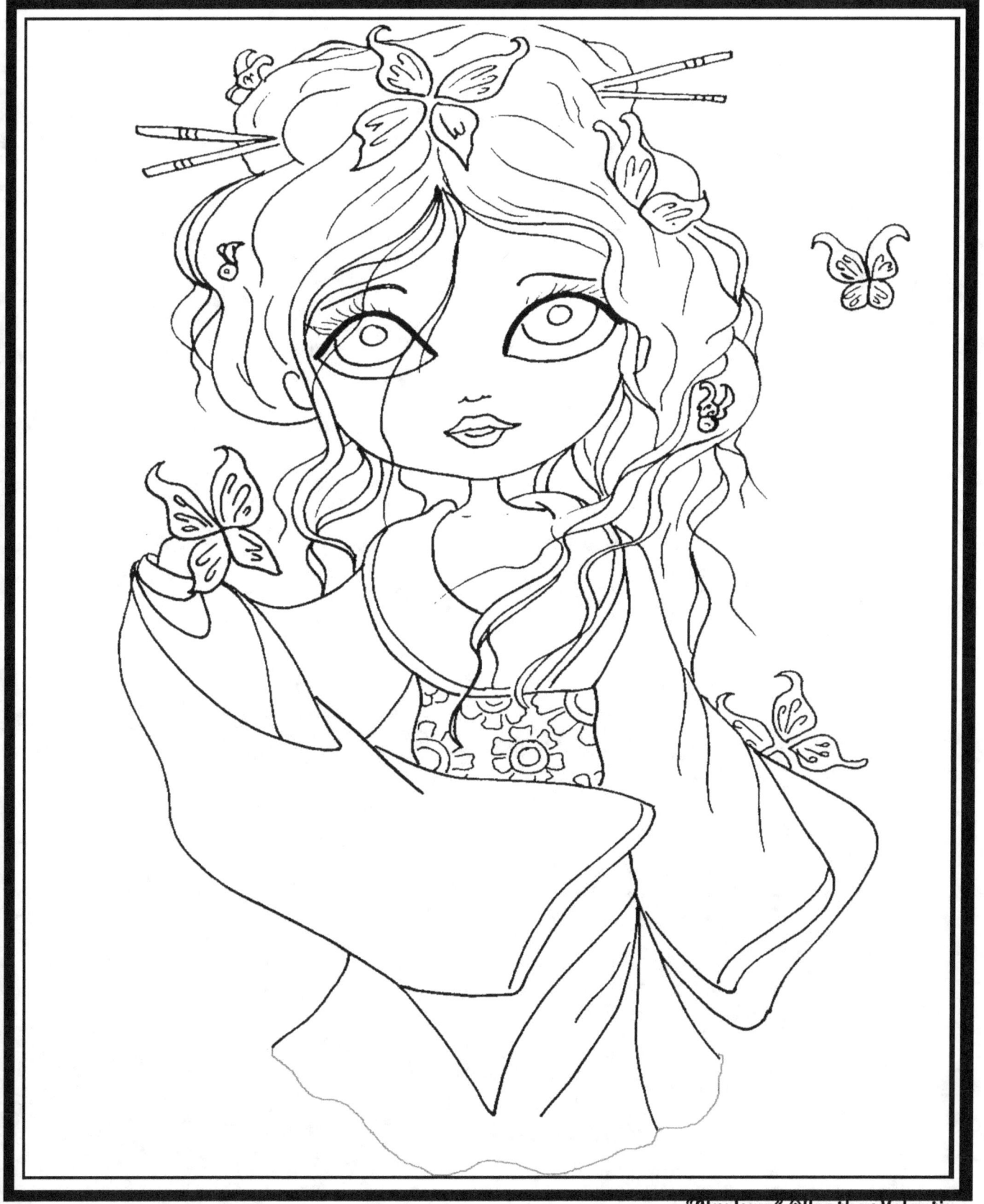

"Sky Lynn" ©Heather Valentin

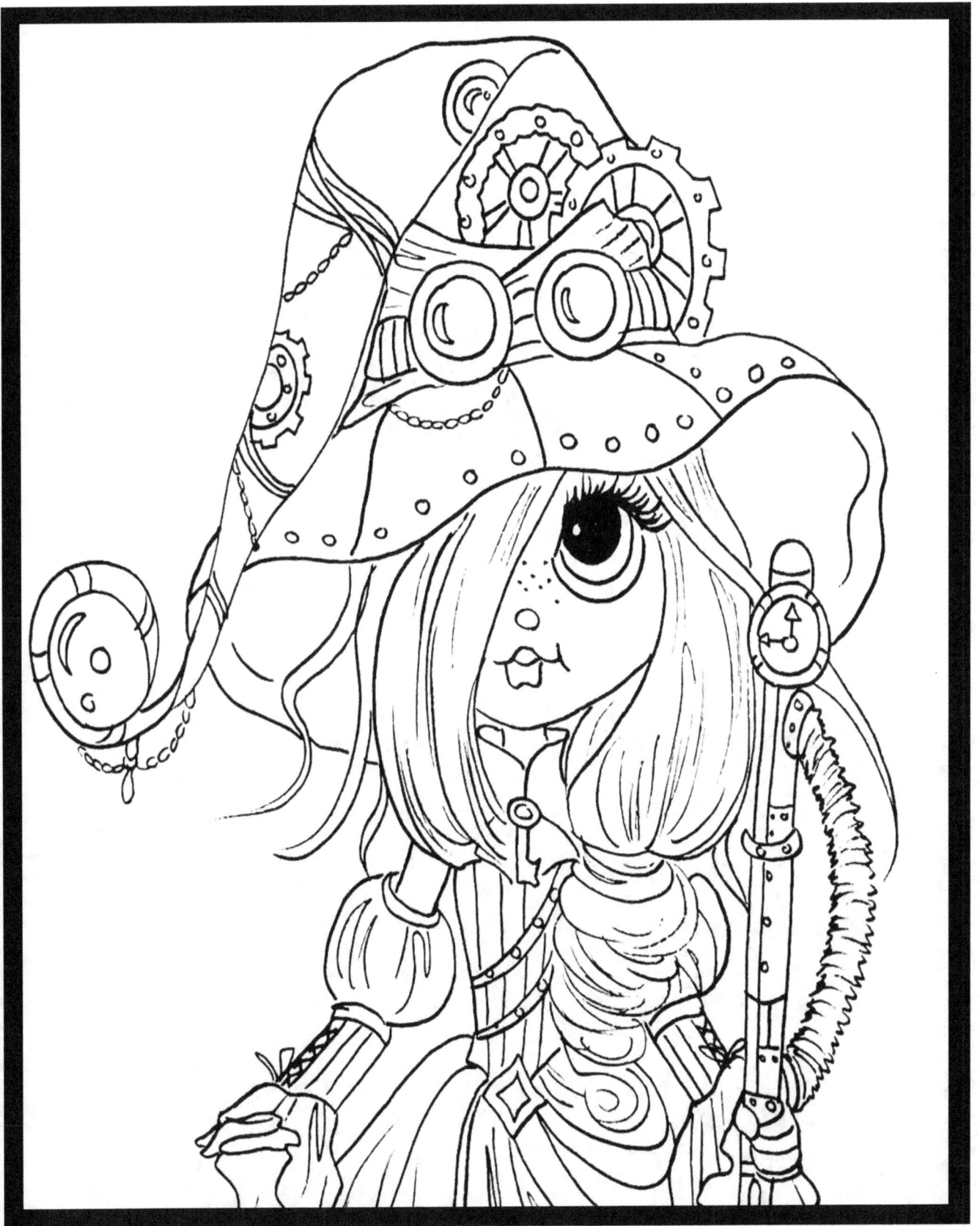

"Rory Witch" by Heather Valentin

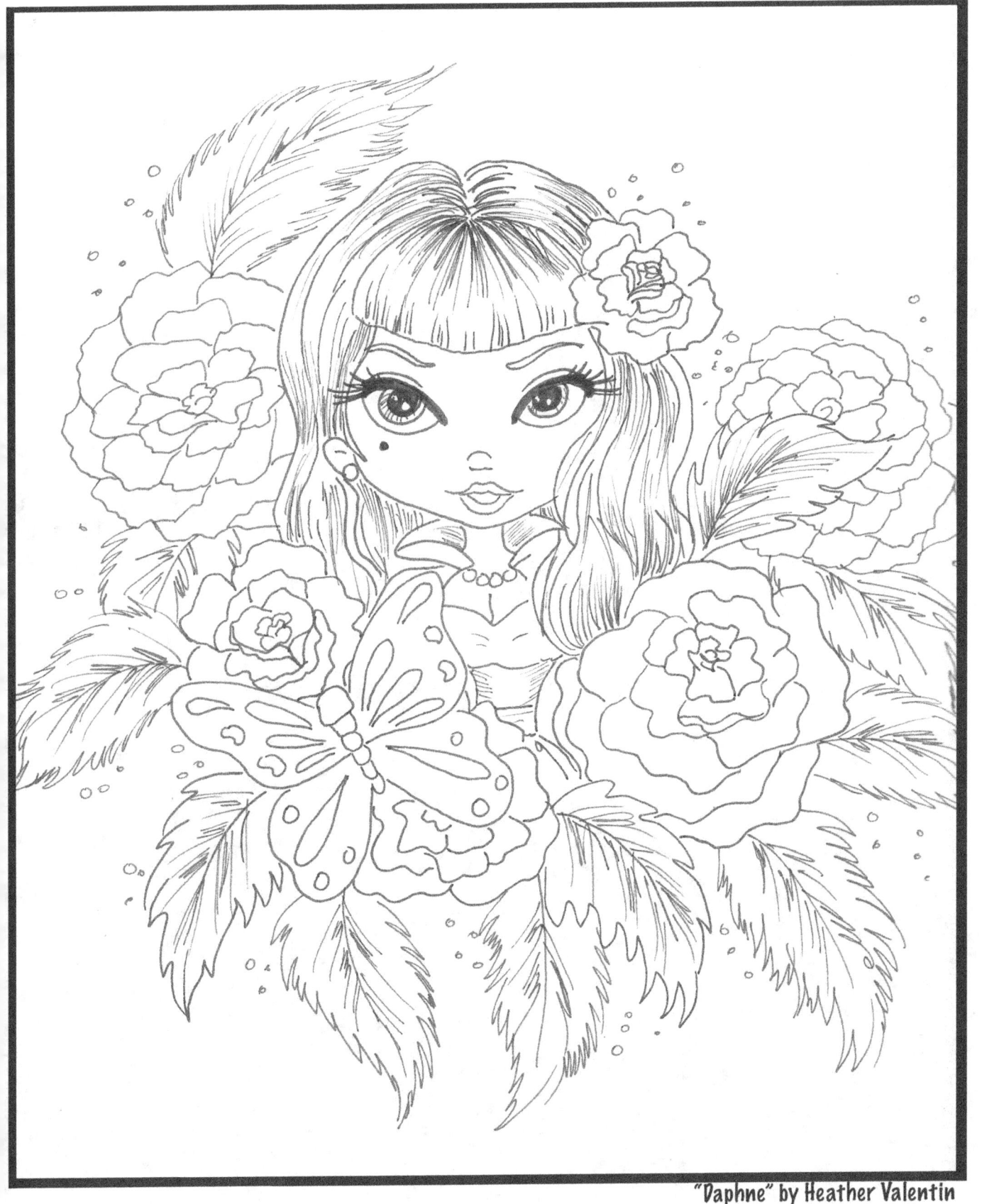

"Daphne" by Heather Valentin

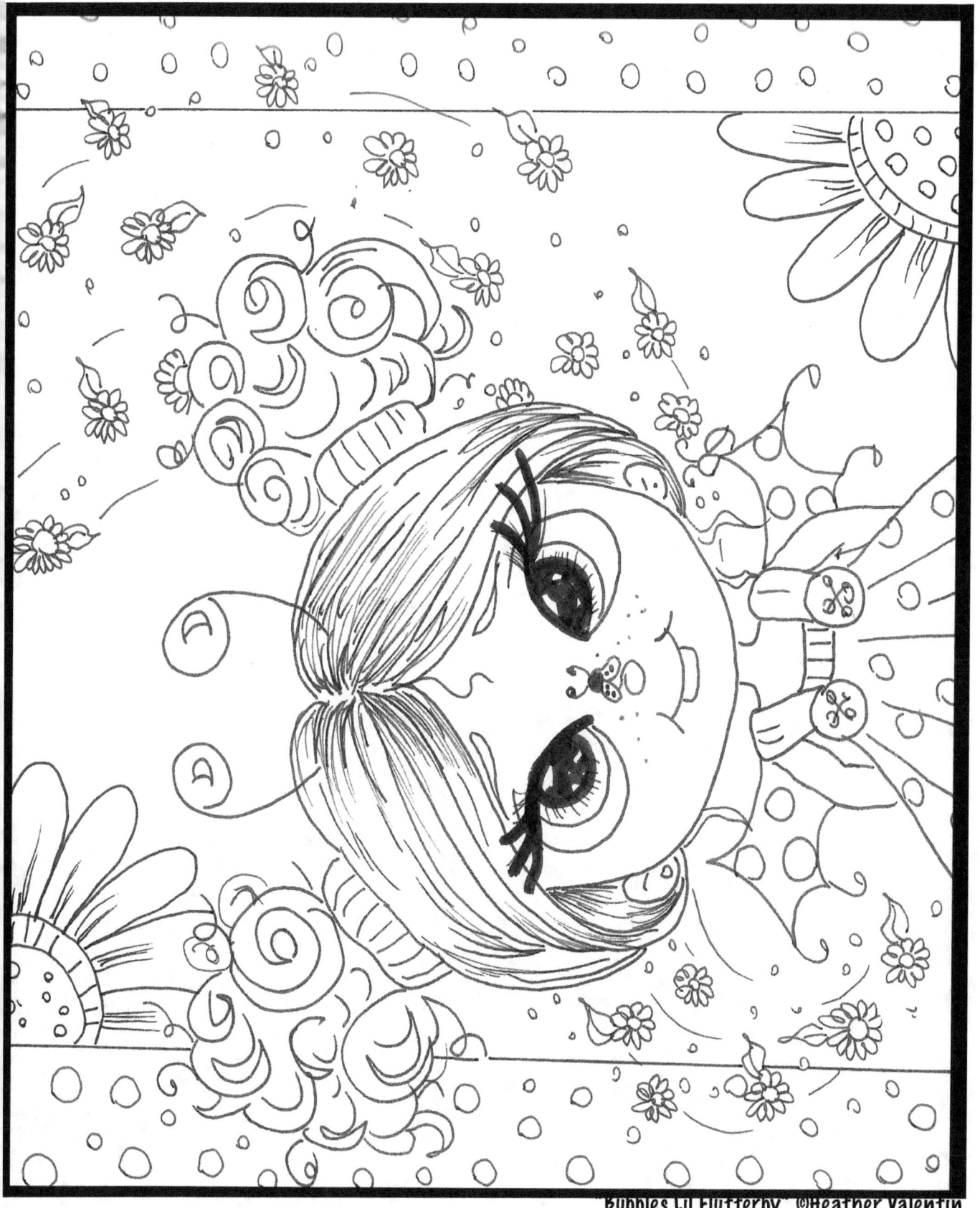

Bubbles Lil Flutterby ©Heather Valentin

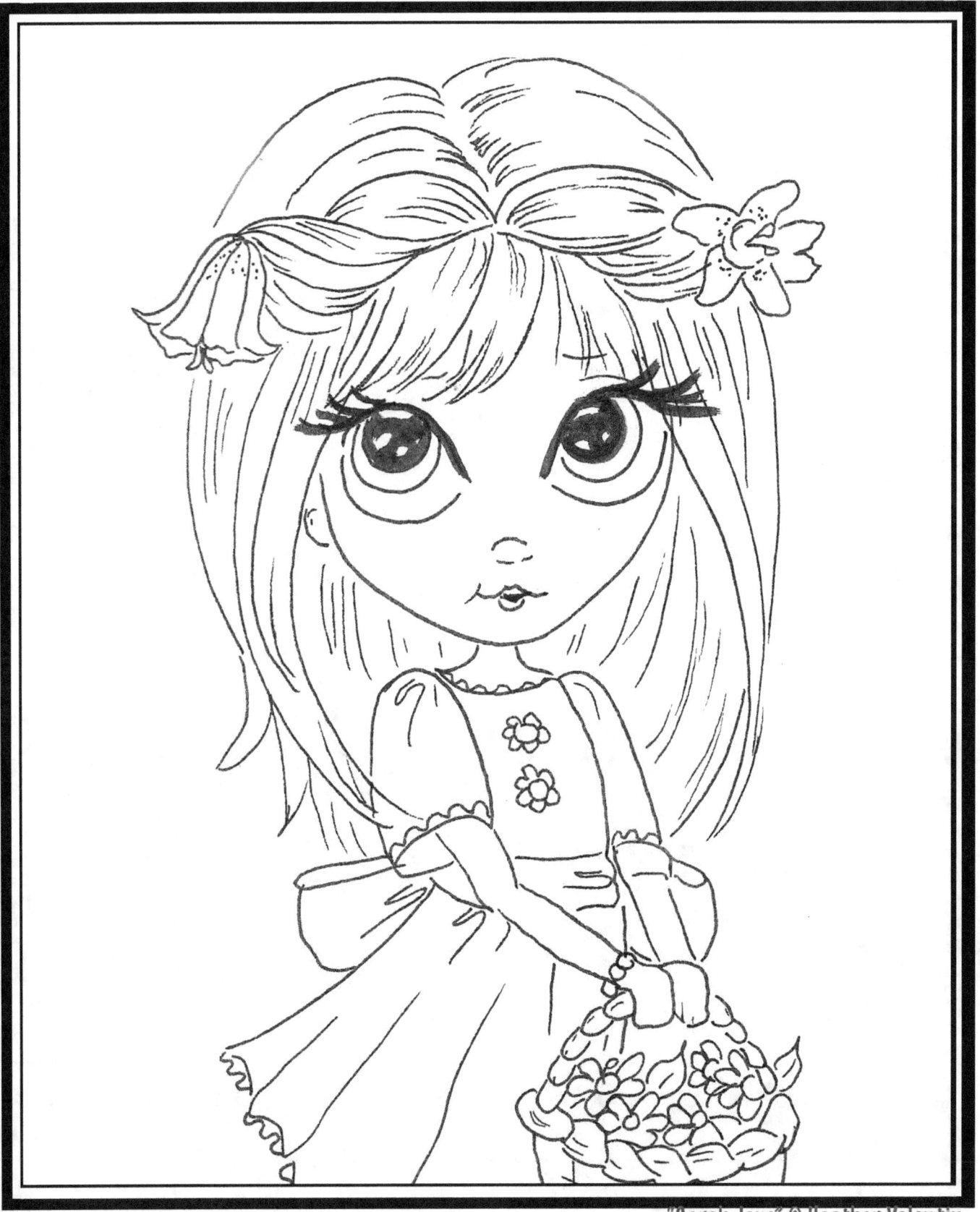

"Sarah Jane" © Heather Valentin

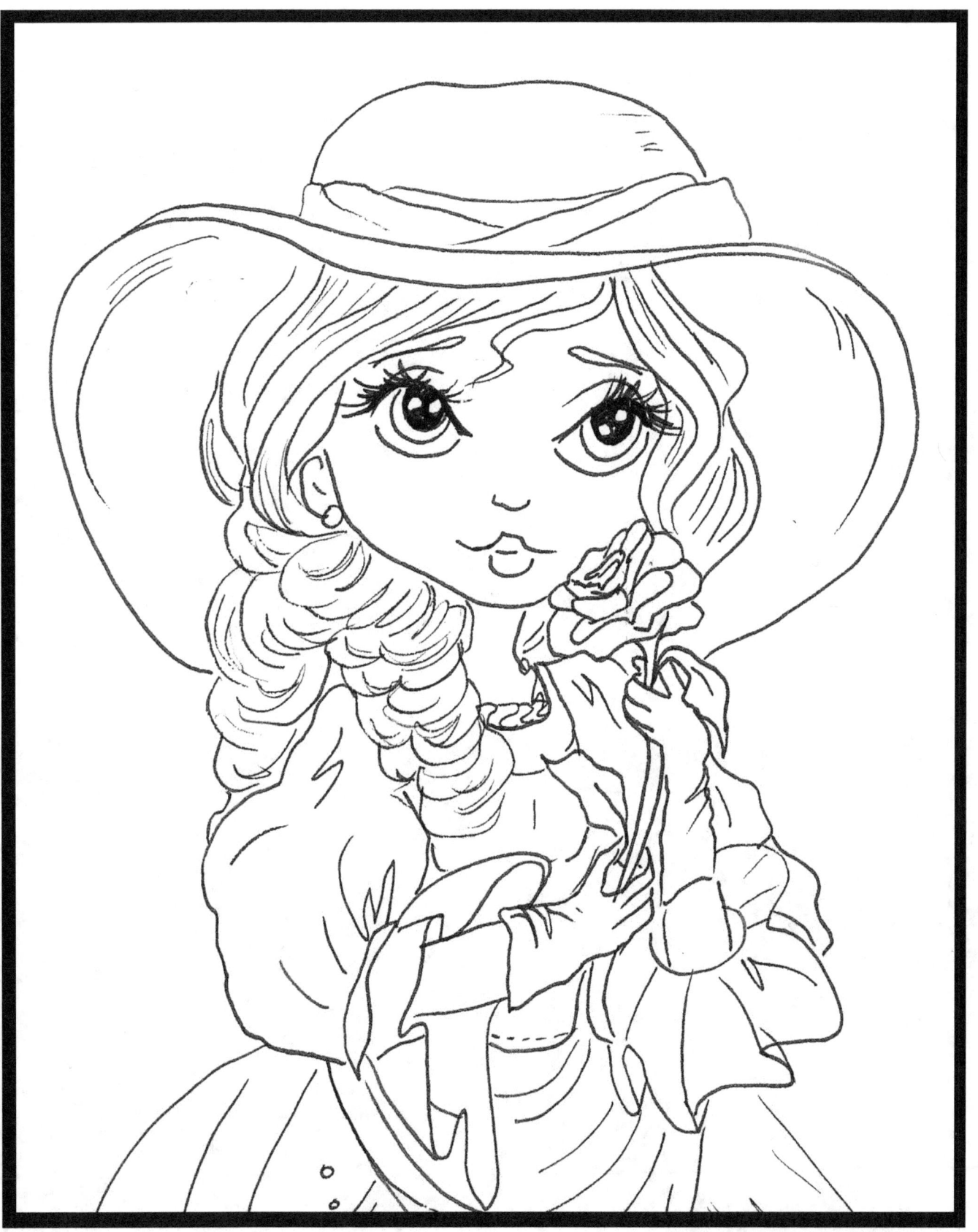

"Emily Rose" by Heather Valentin

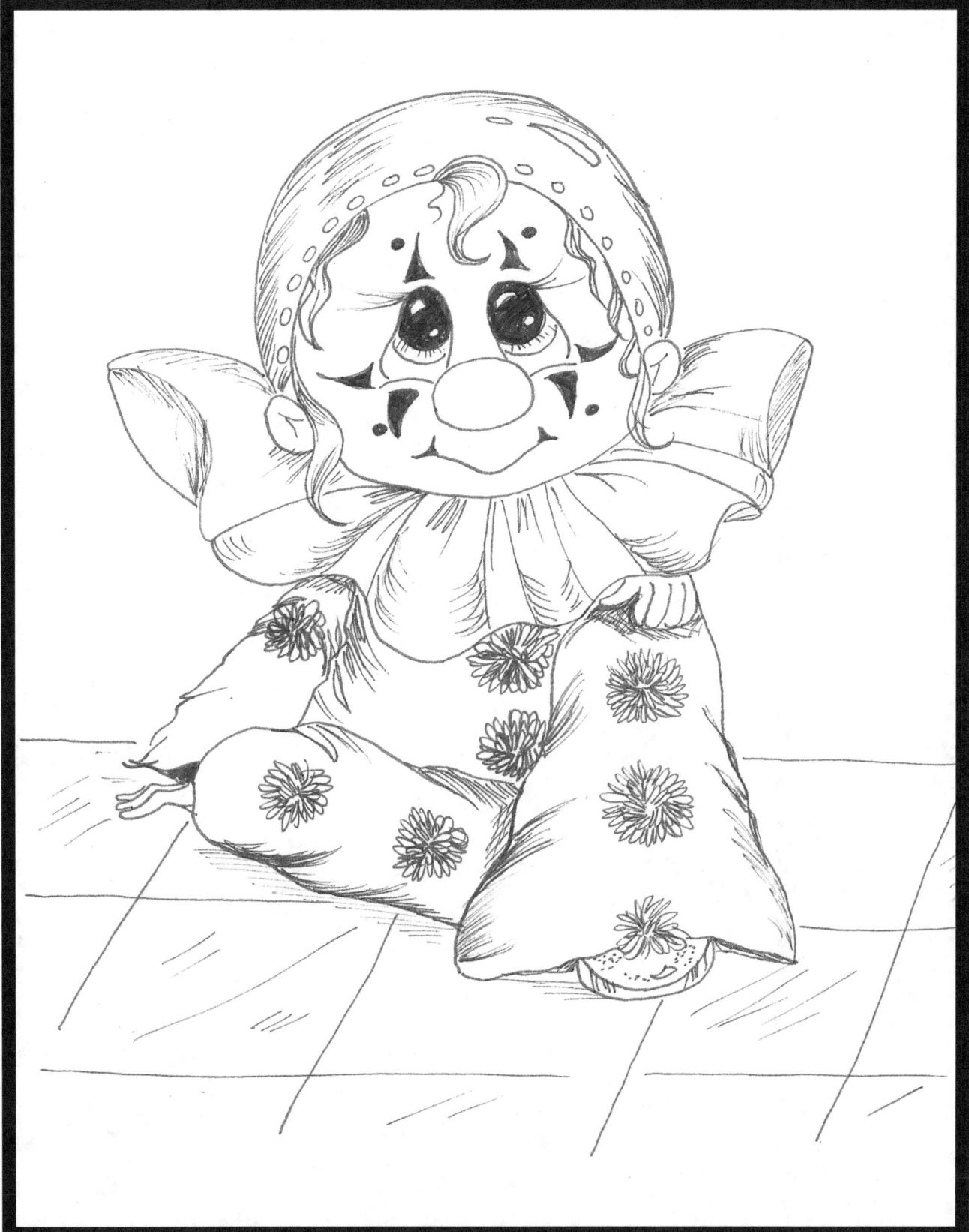

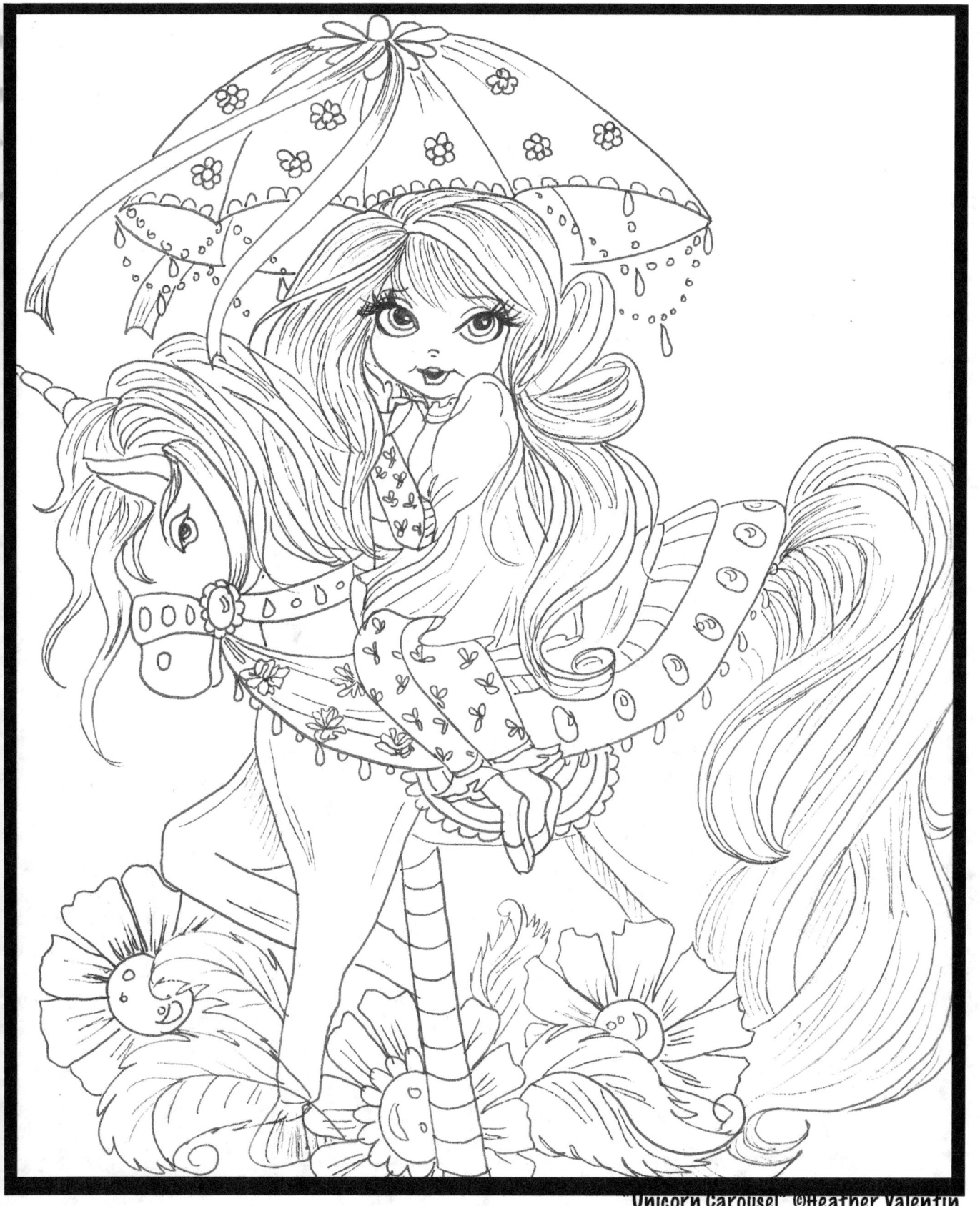

Unicorn Carousel ©Heather Valentin

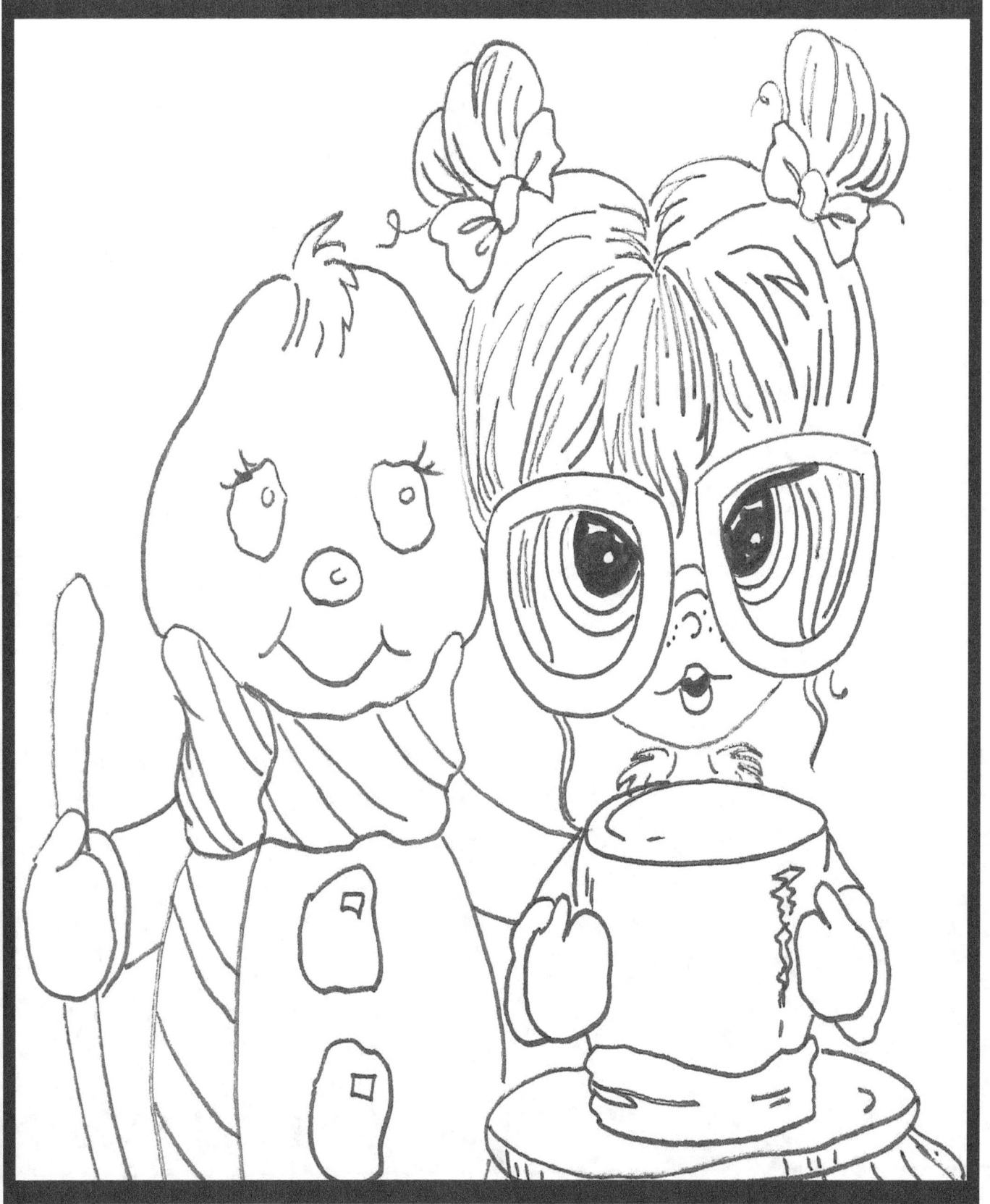

"Eleanor and The Snowman" by Heather Valentin

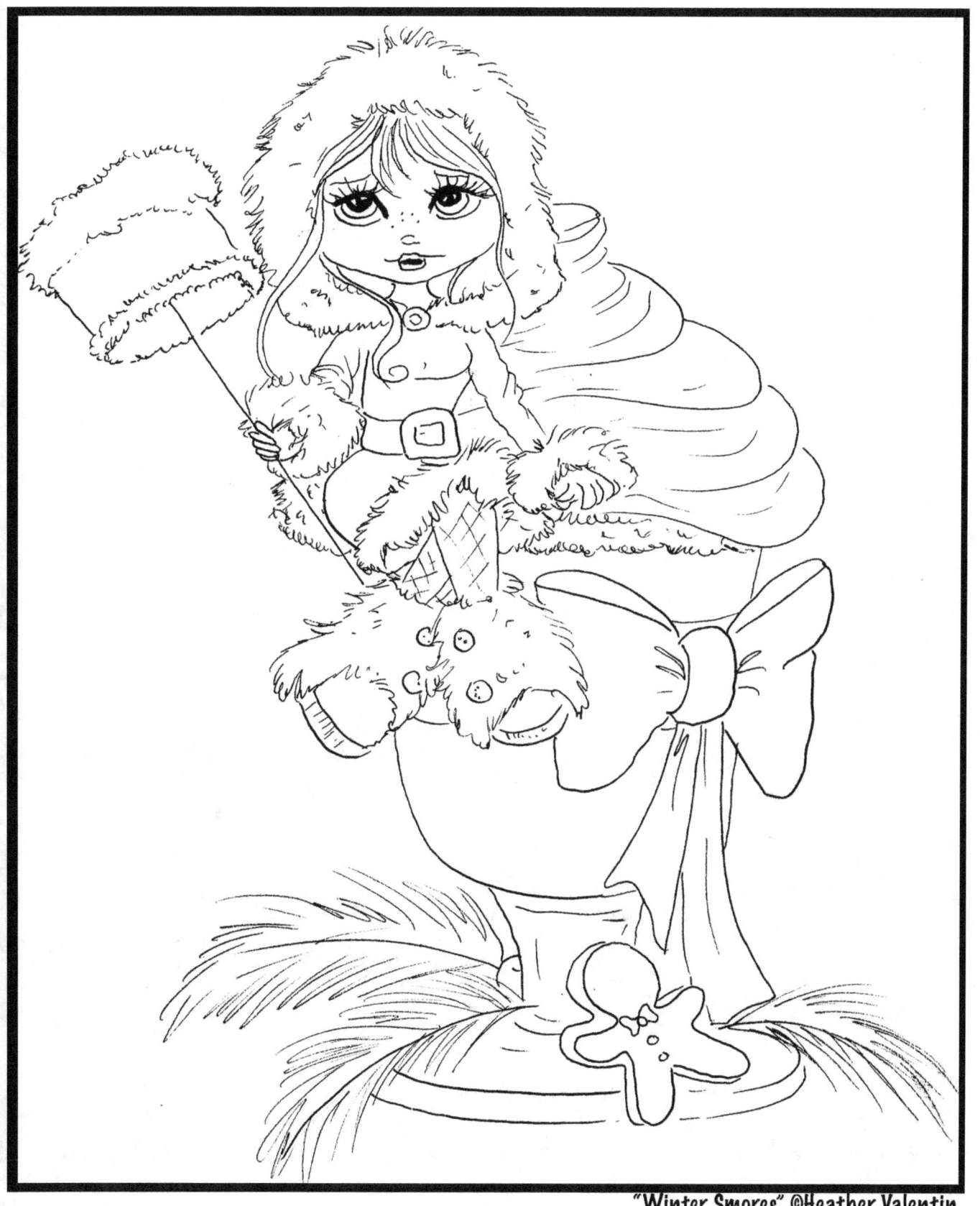

"Winter Smores" ©Heather Valentin

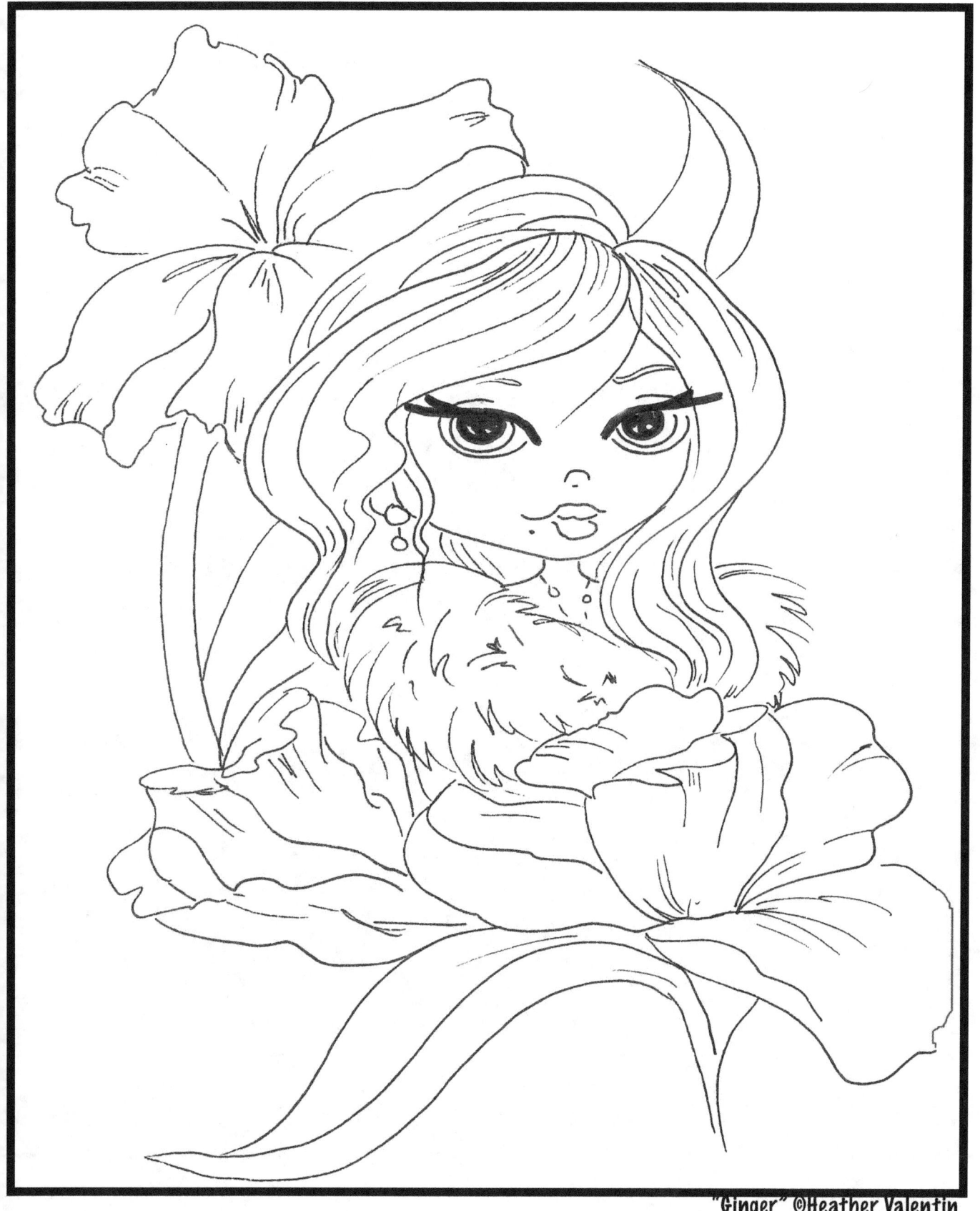

"Ginger" ©Heather Valentin

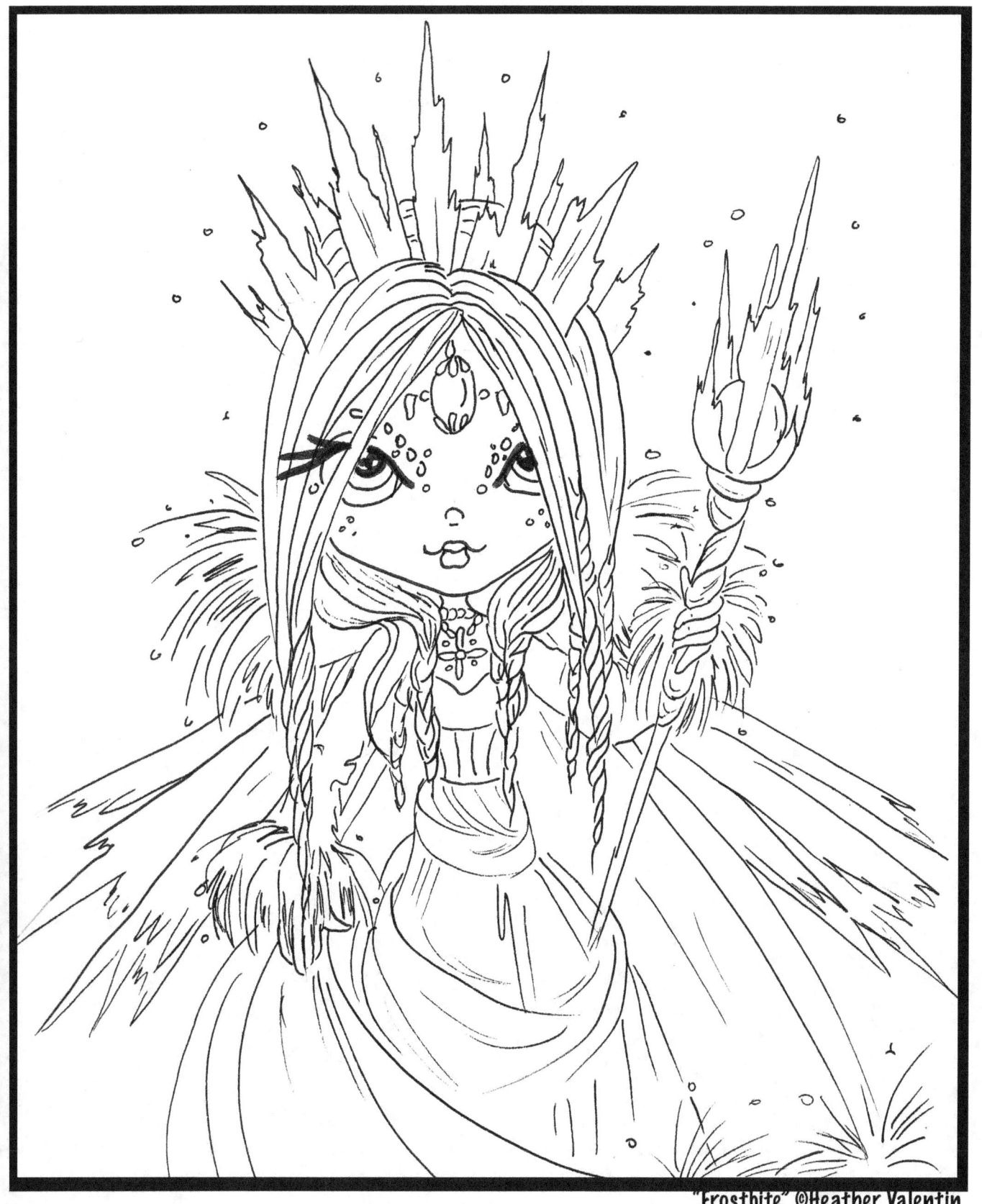

"Frostbite" ©Heather Valentin

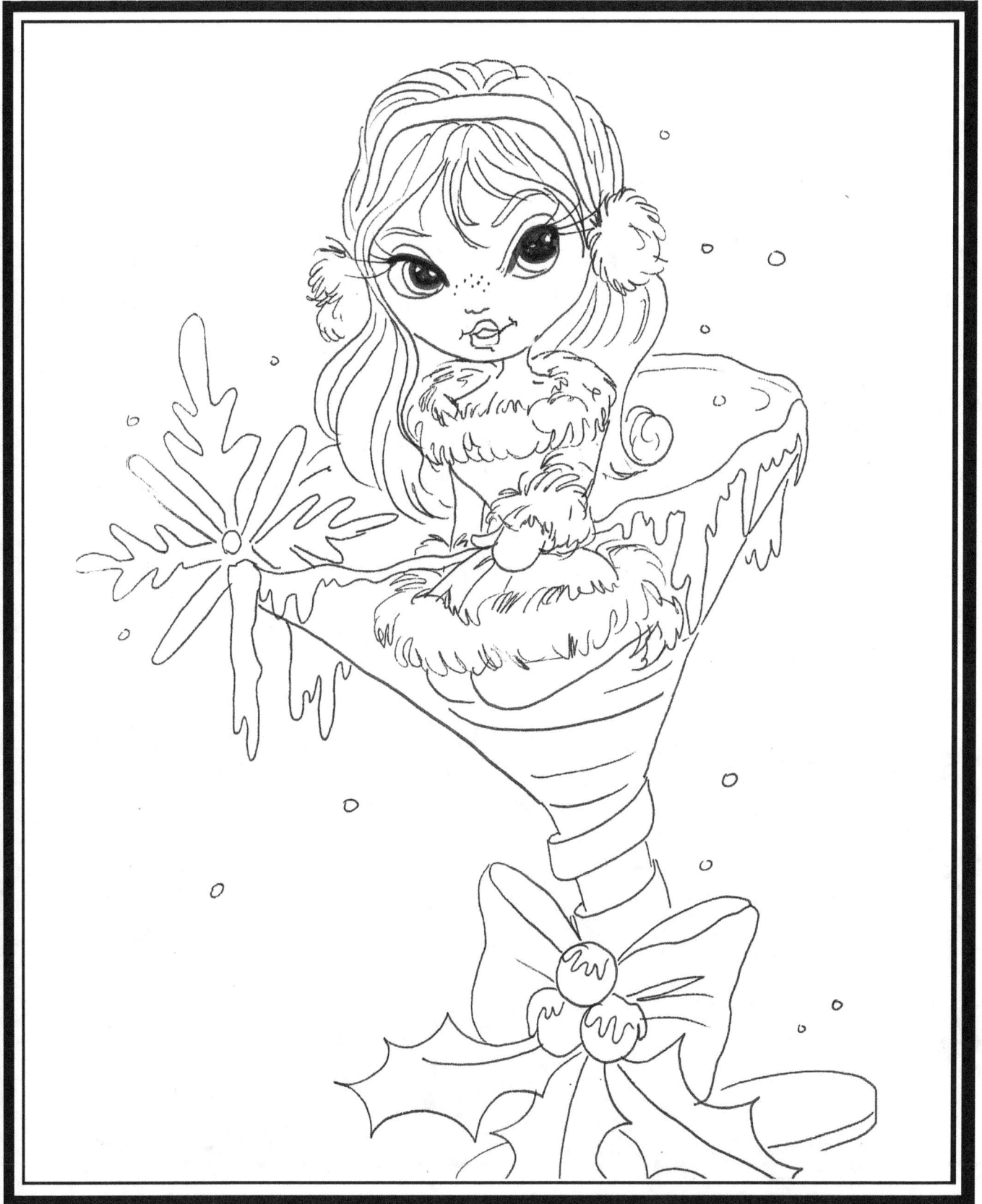

"Sparletini" ©Heather Valentin

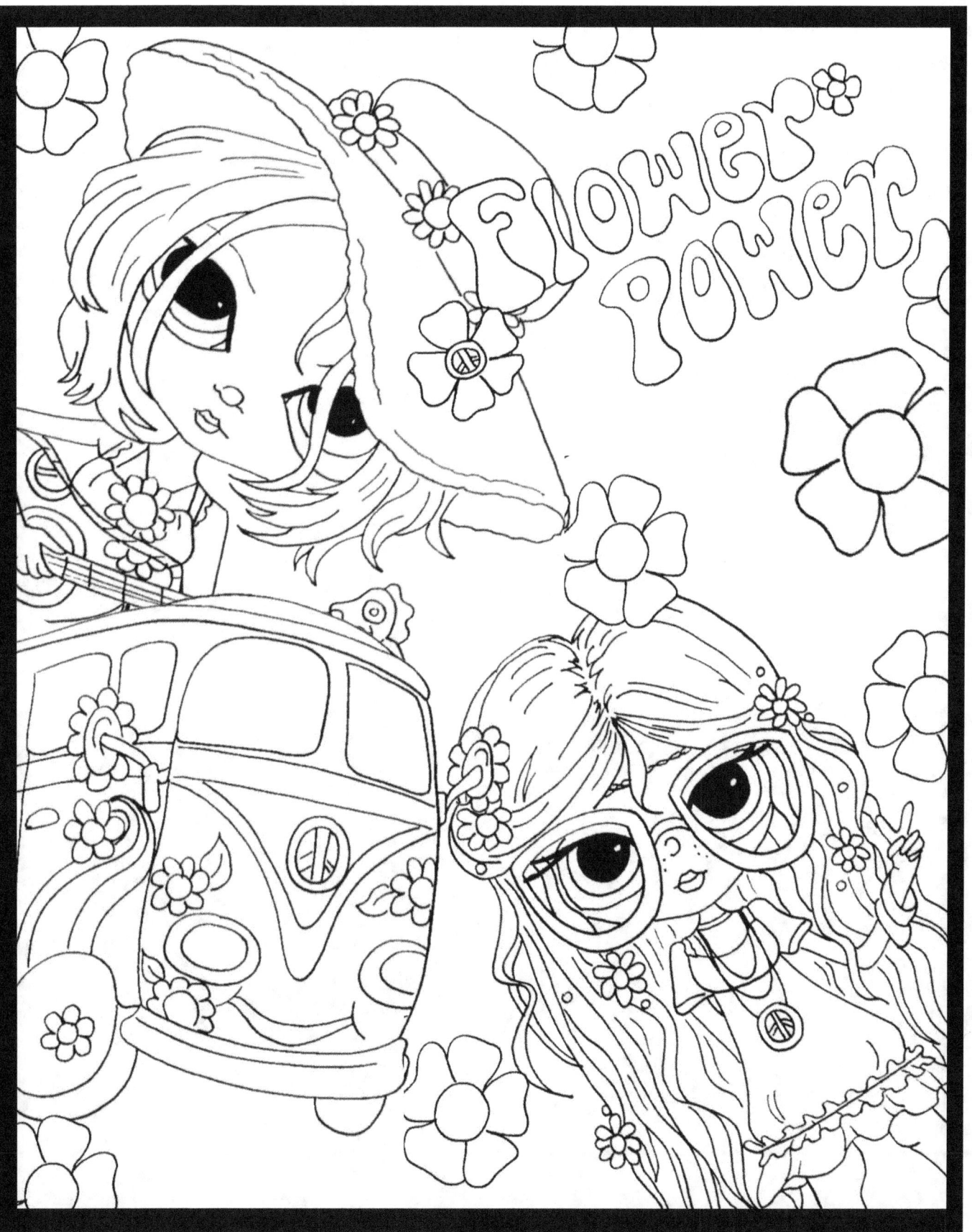

"Maddie and Eleanor Flower Power" by Heather Valentin

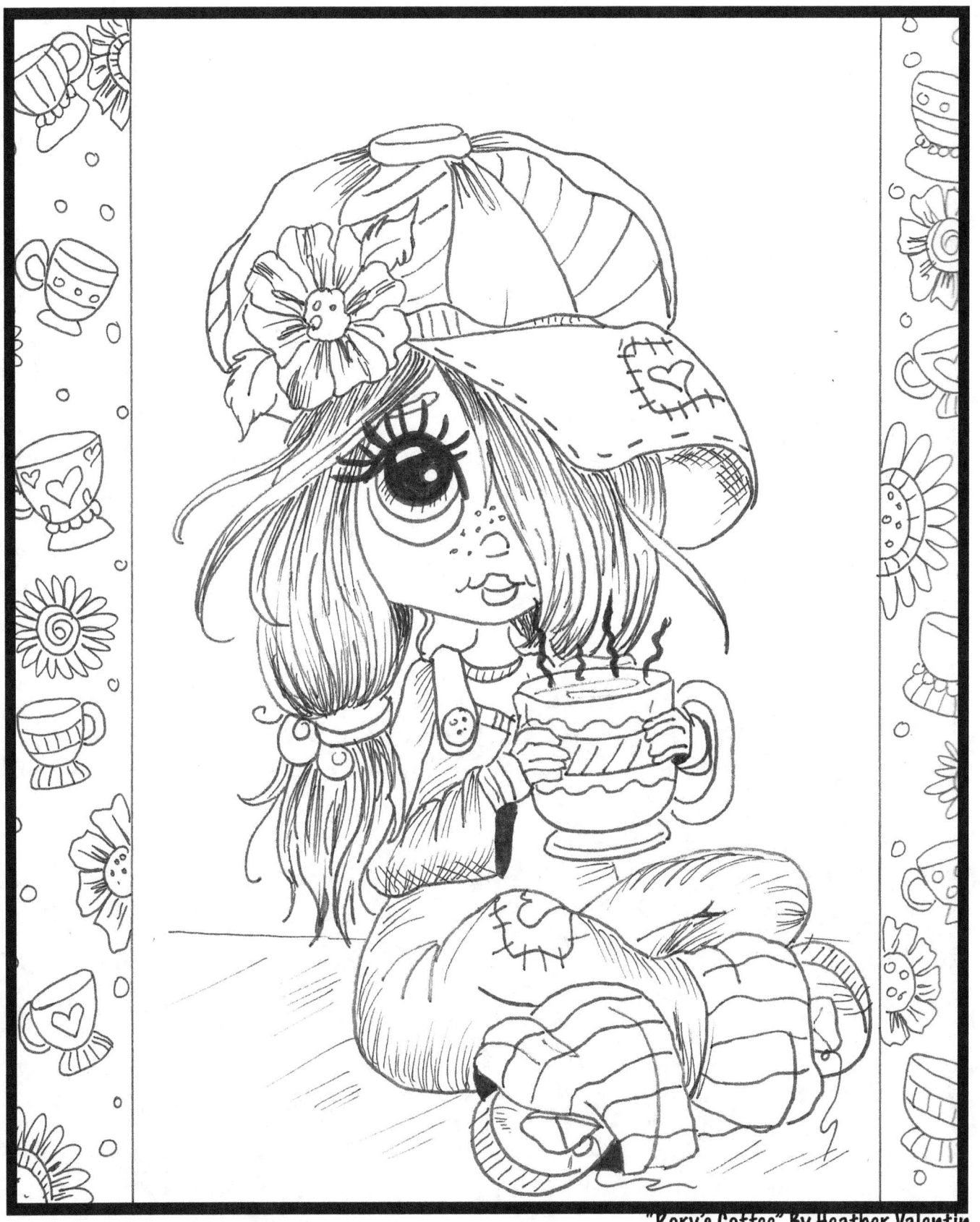

"Kory's Coffee" By Heather Valentin

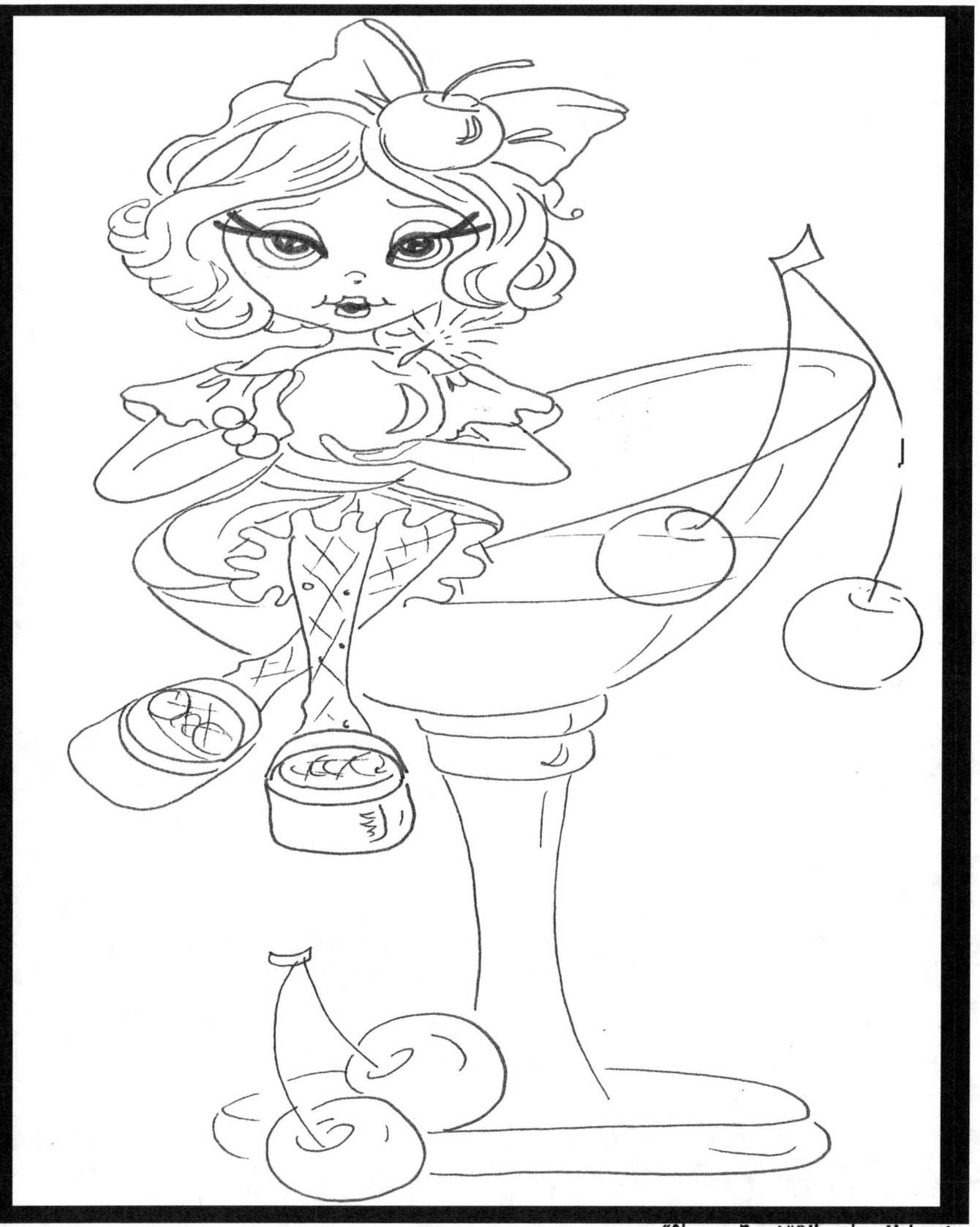

"Cherry Bomb"©Heather Valentin

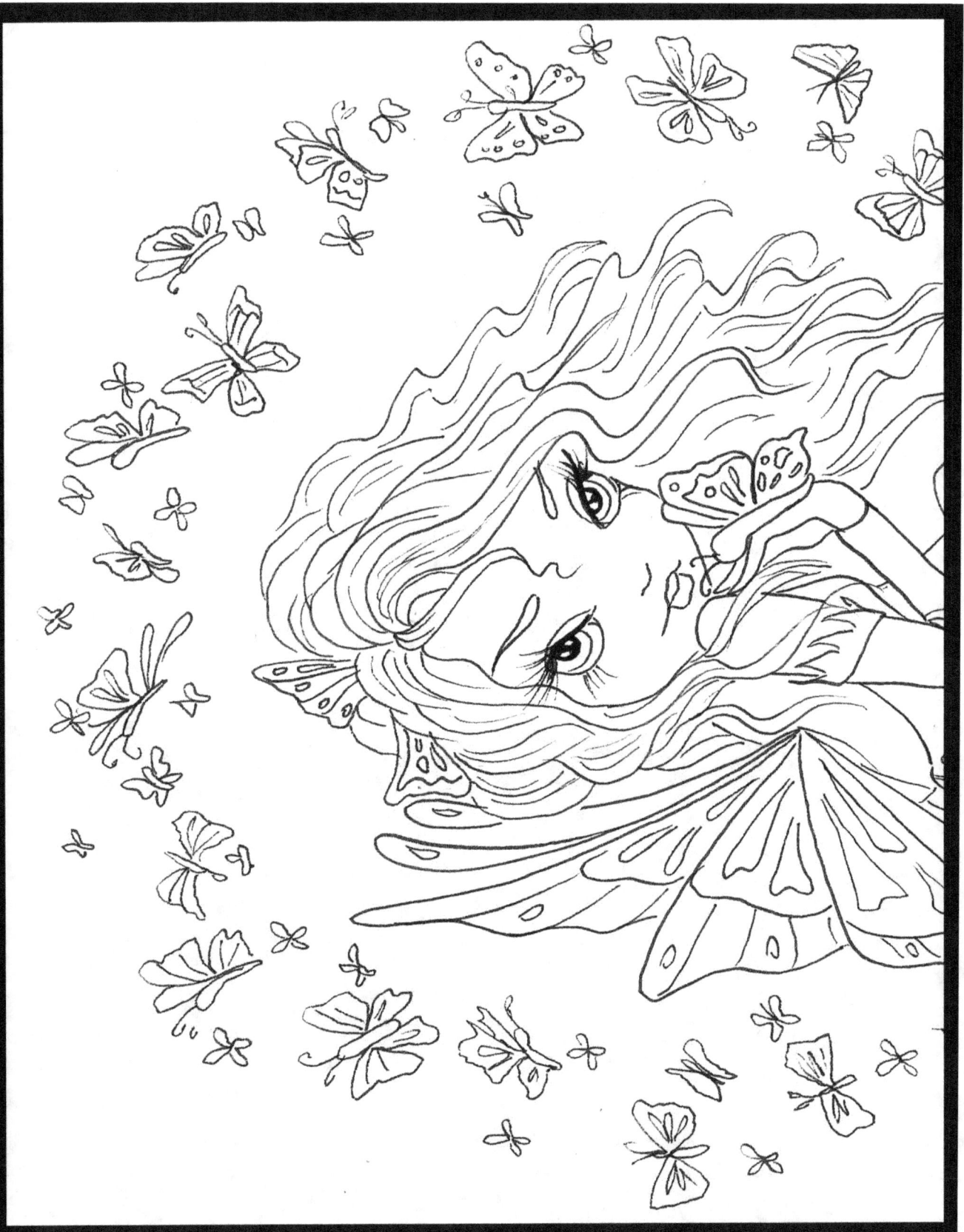

"Aveline" by Heather Valentin

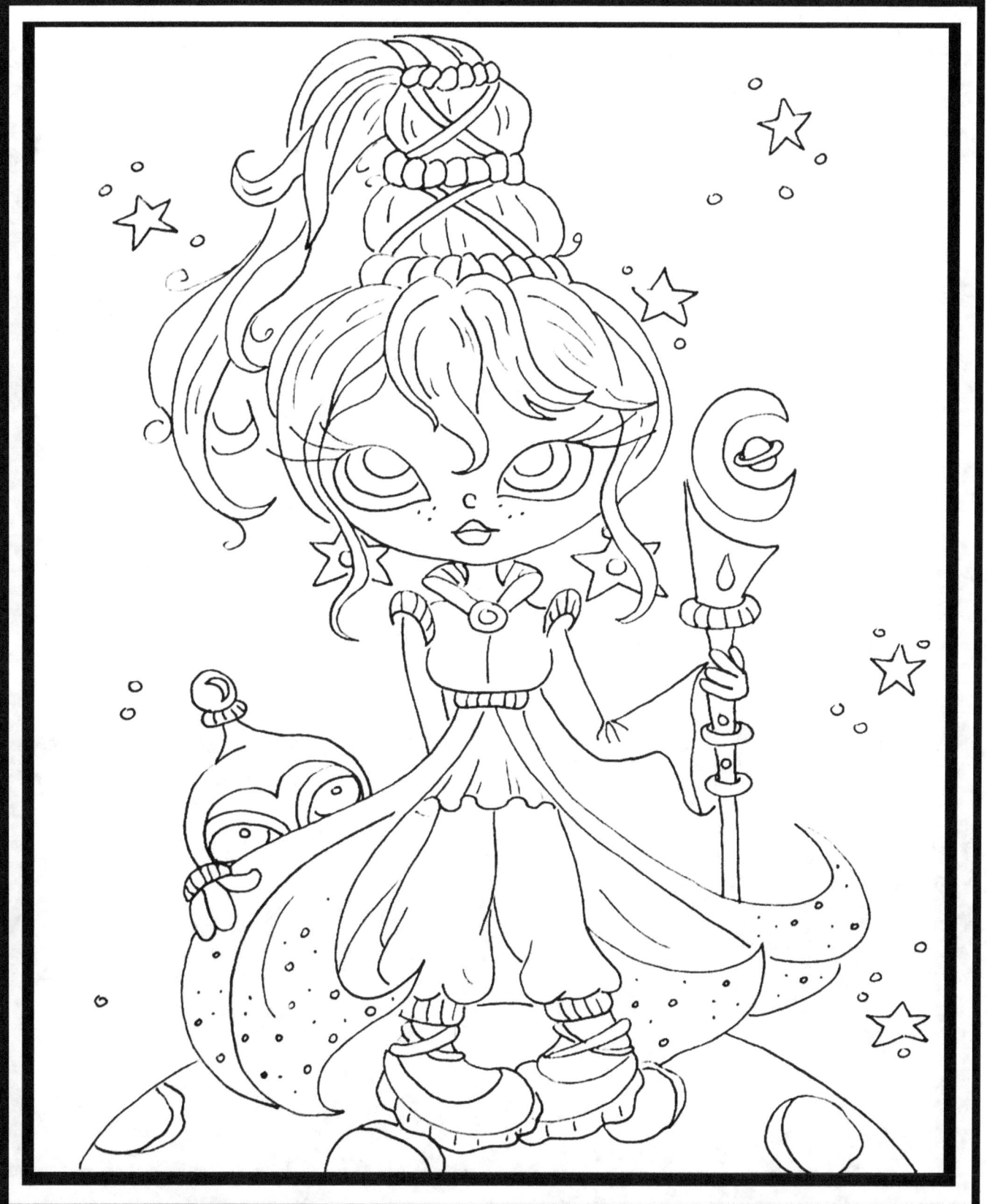

"Space Queen"©Heather Valentin

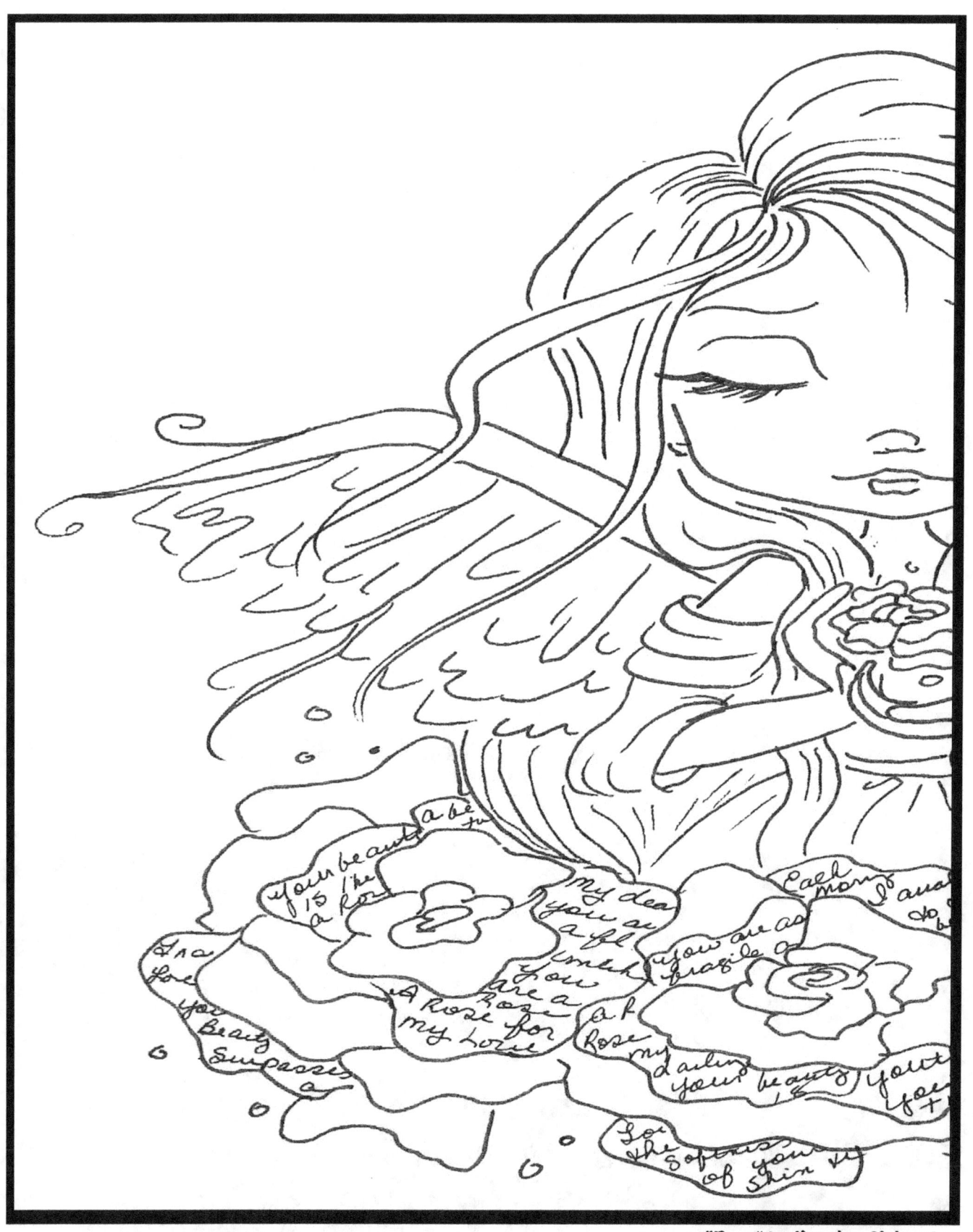

"Rose" by Heather Valentin

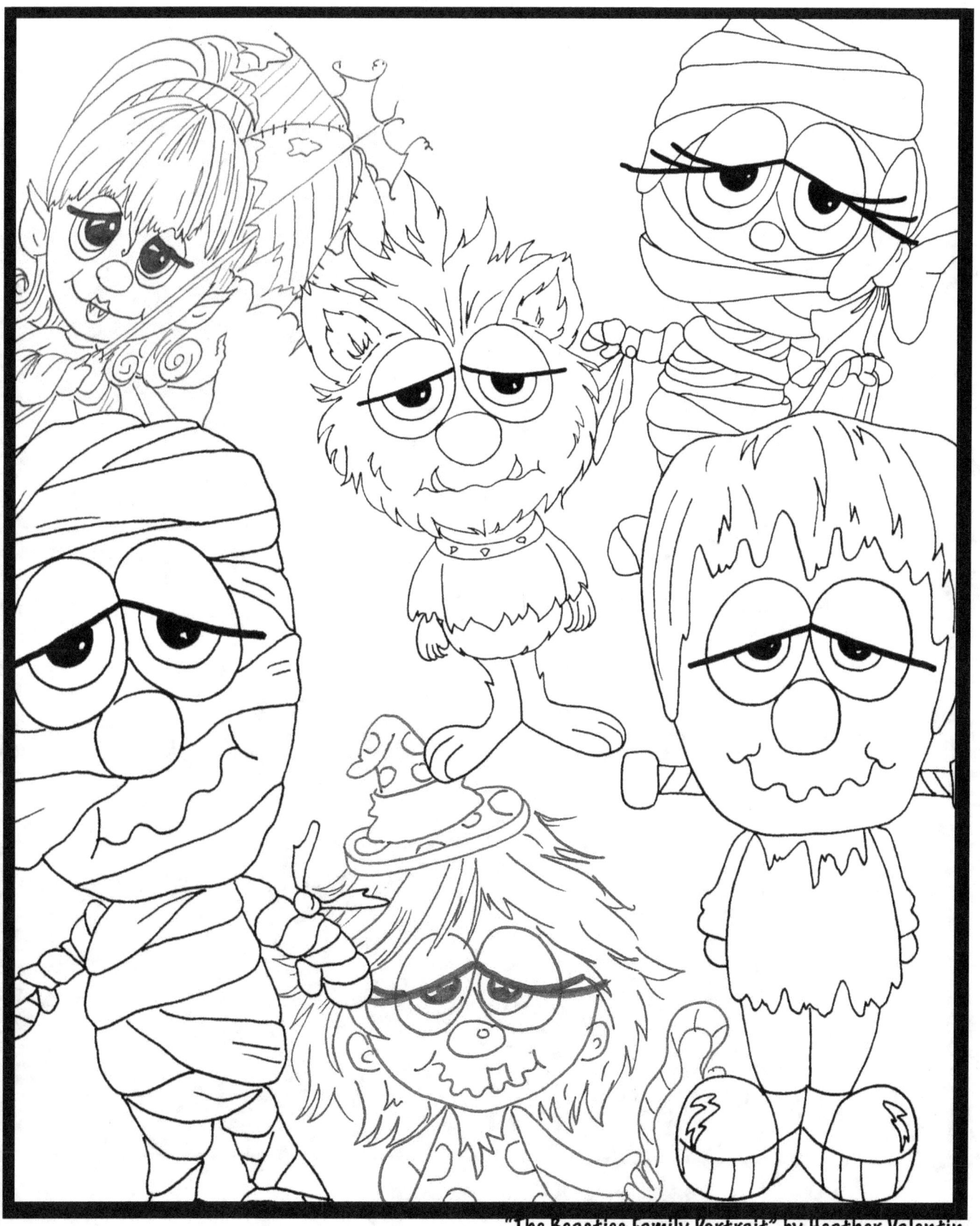

"The Beasties Family Portrait" by Heather Valentin

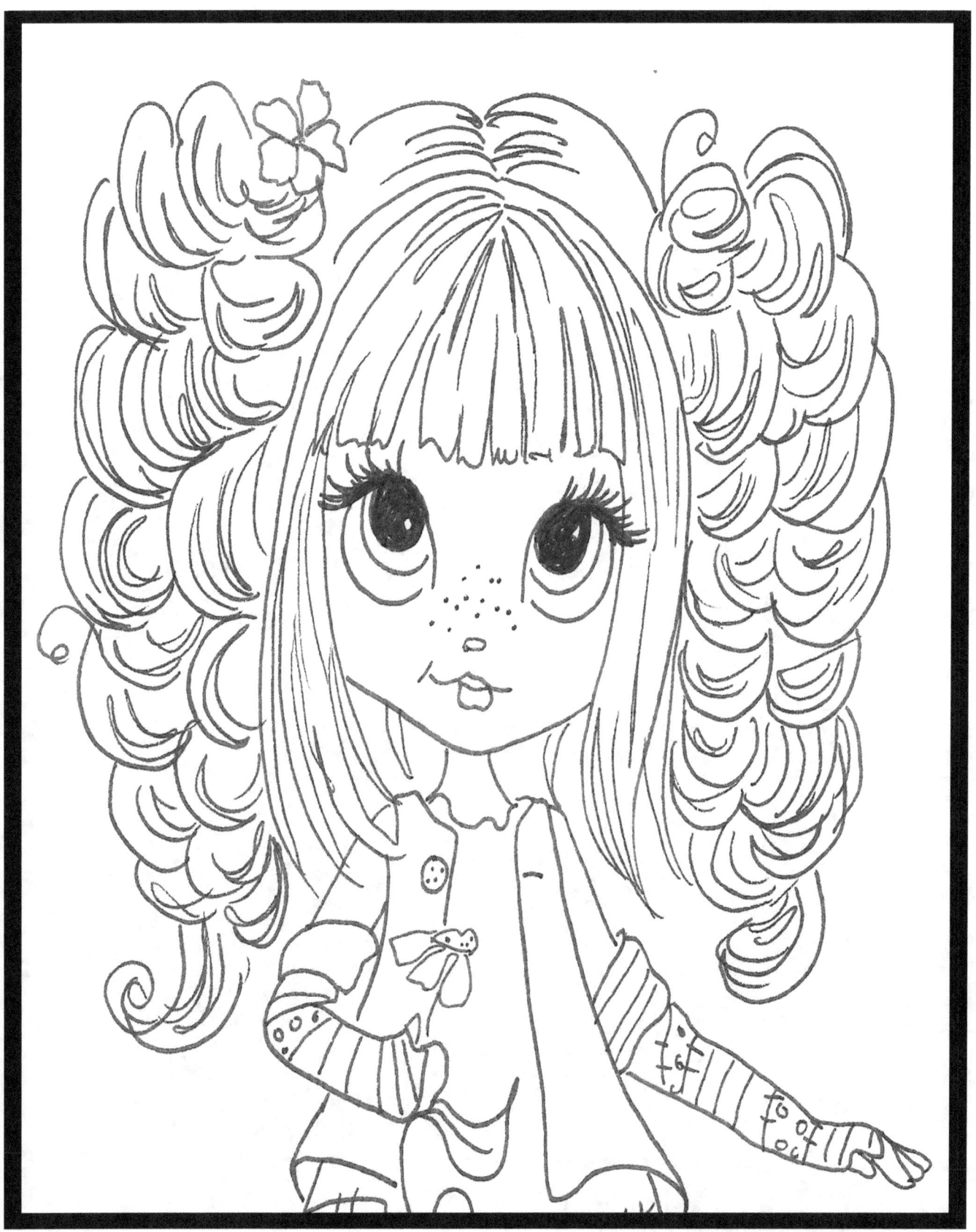

"Violet" by Heather Valentin

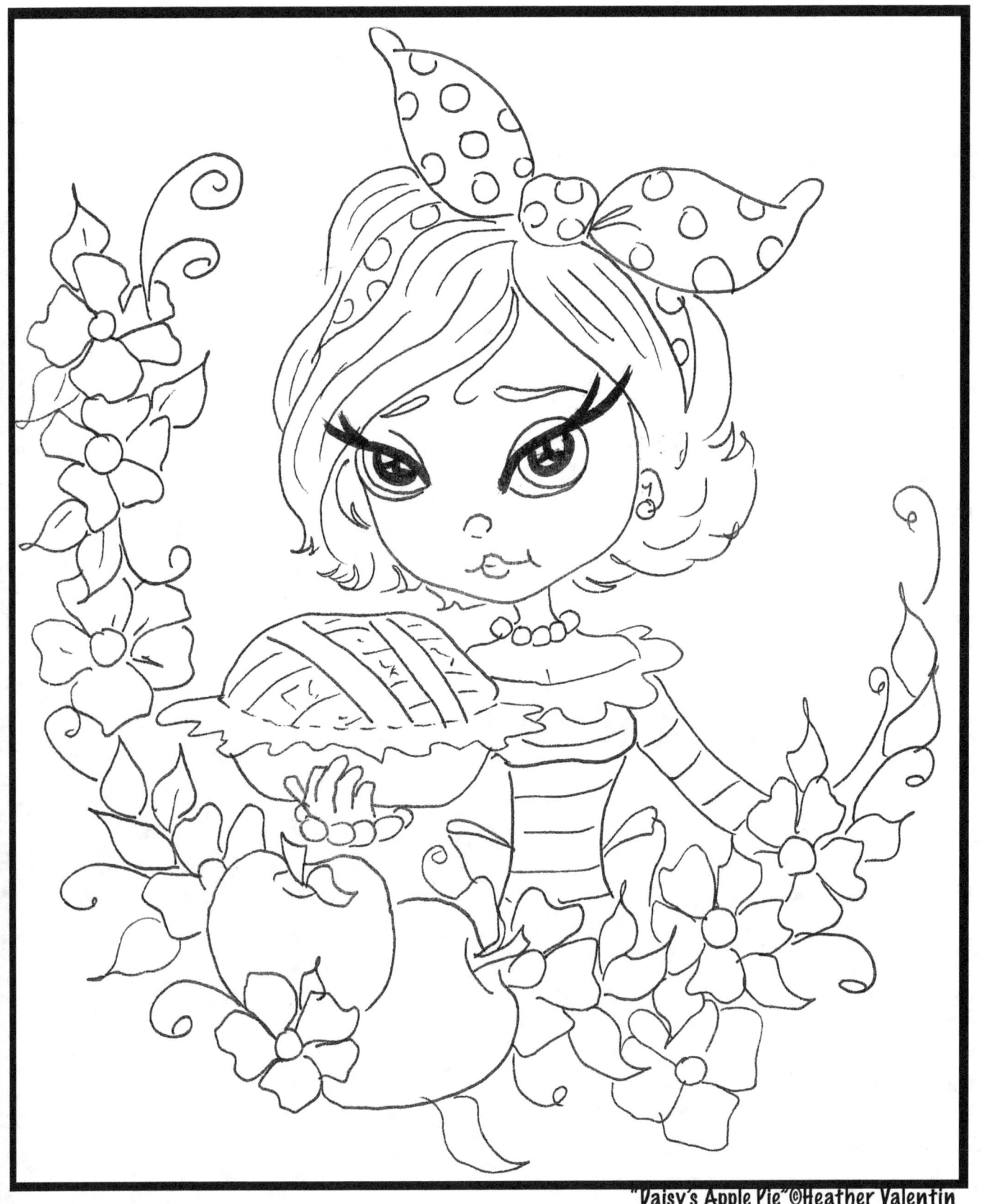

"Daisy's Apple Pie"©Heather Valentin

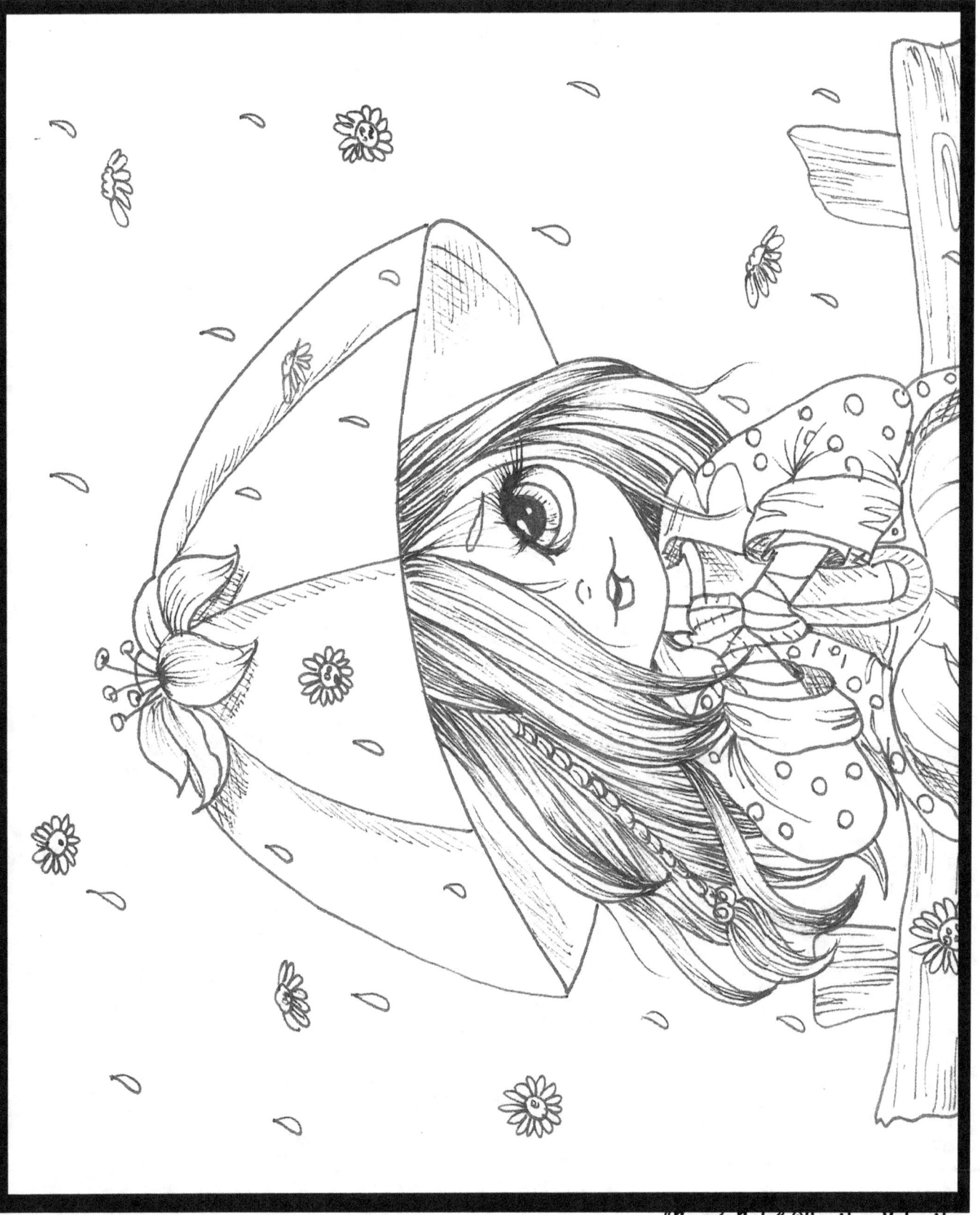

"Kory's Rain" ©Heather Valentin

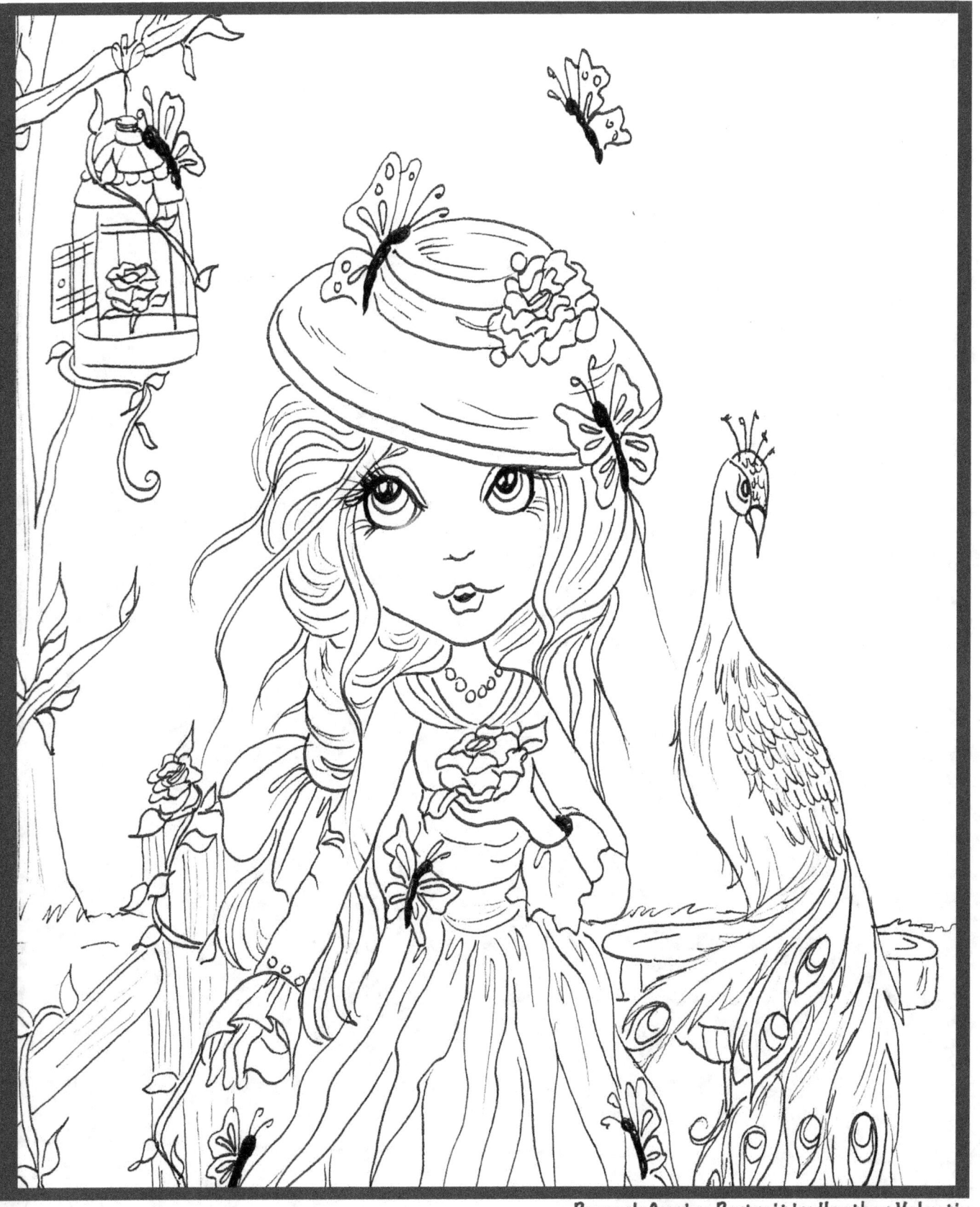

Peacock Garden Portrait by Heather Valentin

Sneak Peek of the soon to be released
Sunshine Tots Coloring Book.

Meet Pinky and Buttercup Sunshine Tot
(Pinky is Buttercup's Pet Dinosaur)

AND

Another sneak peek of the soon to be released
Sunshine Elves Coloring Book.

Meet Starlyte.

Enjoy! As always... Color. Create. Dream and
Believe ....Lacy Sunshine.
Hugs, Heather

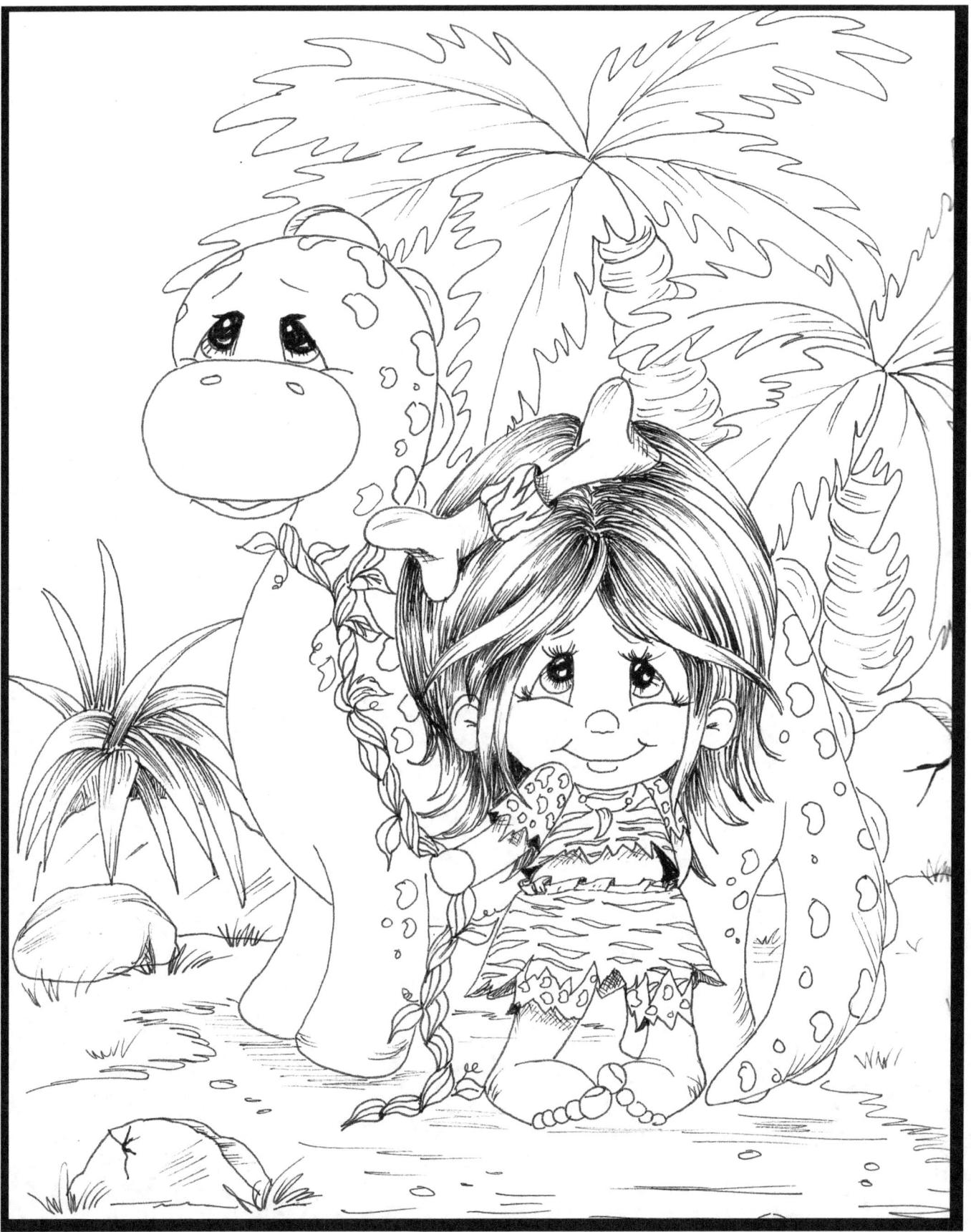

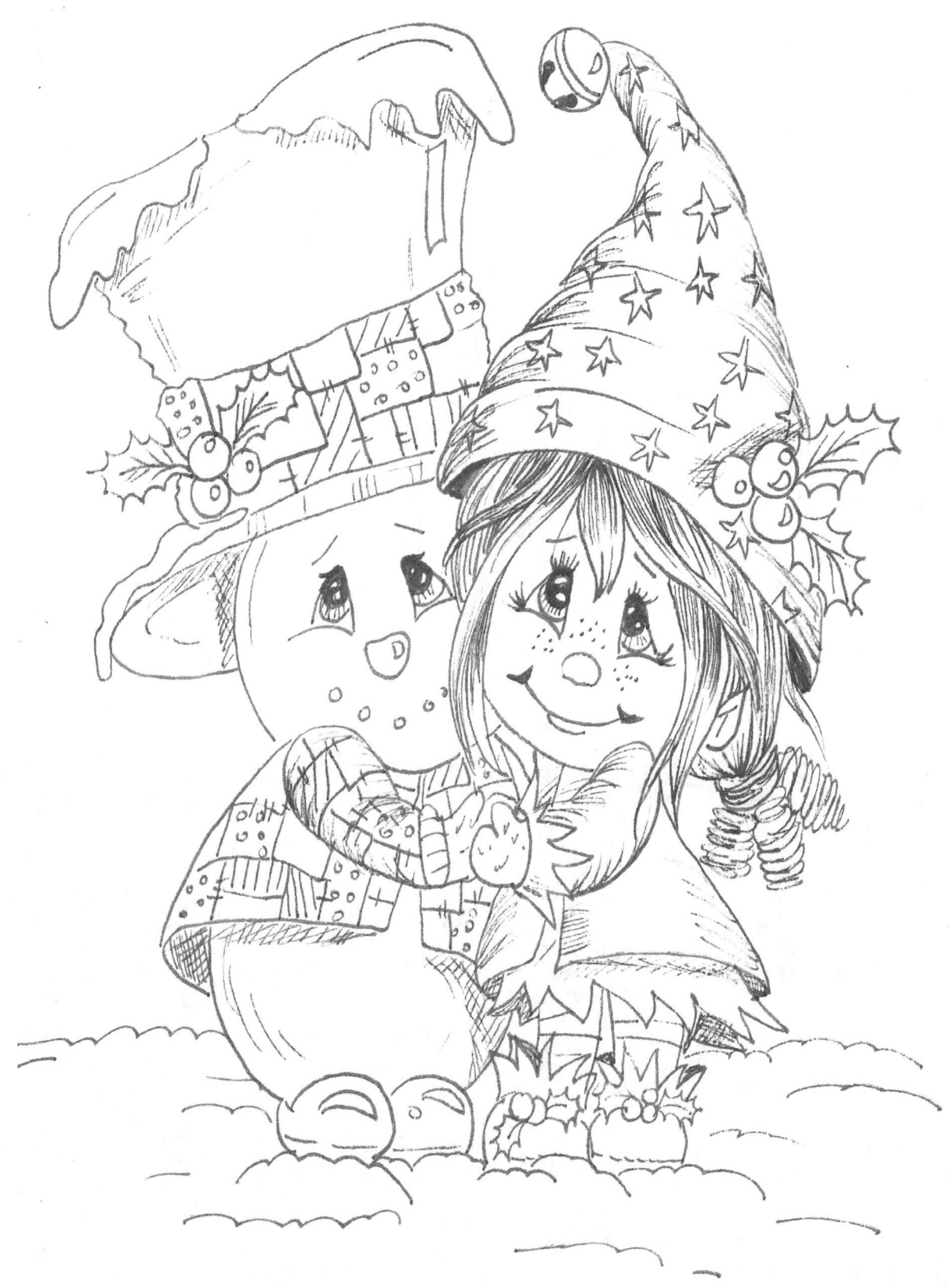

www.ingramcontent.com/pod-product-compliance
Lightning Source LLC
Chambersburg PA
CBHW081748220526
45468CB00008B/2287